S0-BYD-224

What you are about to read will challenge everything you have ever thought about the world of animals.

Here you will see abilities that you previously believed could only be demonstrated by very special humans—amazing case histories like the dog that predicted presidential elections, the end of New York subway strike, and the outcome of the seventh game of the 1966 World Series!

The Psychic Power of Animals

is a landmark work in psychic phenomena—a spellbinding book that will astound and fascinate you.

Fawcett Gold Medal Books
by Bill Schul:

THE SECRET POWER OF PYRAMIDS *(with Ed Petti)*

THE PSYCHIC POWER OF ANIMALS

The Psychic
Power
of Animals

Bill Schul

FAWCETT GOLD MEDAL • NEW YORK

A Fawcett Gold Medal Book
Published by Ballantine Books
Copyright © 1977 by Fawcett Publications, Inc.

All rights reserved under International and Pan-American Copyright Conventions, including the right to reproduce this book of portions thereof in any form. Published in the United States by Ballantine Books, a division of Random House, Inc., New York, and simultaneously in Canada by Random House of Canada Limited, Toronto.

ISBN 0-449-13724-4

Manufactured in the United States of America

First Fawcett Gold Medal Printing: August 1977
First Ballantine Books Edition: February 1988

Cover photo © 1987 Walter Chandoha

Contents

To Curly, Baron, Phagen, Ya-Hootie, Babe, Sady,
and all the other creatures large and small who,
in sharing their lives with us, enriched ours immeasurably.

But ask now the beasts,
And they shall teach thee,
And the fowls of the air,
And they shall tell thee.

Job 12:7-10

Introduction

I have always felt a certain sadness for those who have never experienced the delight and wonder of animals.

Someone who has never shared with a puppy the abandon and sheer joy of just being alive, who has never crouched beside the bed of a mother cat and her newborn kittens, watched the daily progress of swallows building their new spring home, helped a still-damp colt take its first wobbling steps, marveled at the beauty of the great Canadian geese on their semiannual flights, spent time alone in the wild country, slept under the stars and listened to the night world of animals, known the deep, abiding love of a pet, shed tears when an old companion and friend has passed on . . . for this person an important part of this world has passed him by.

For those who have shared their lives with furred, feathered, and scaled fellow dwellers on this planet, this book will tend to confirm their likely already held convictions that animals are marvelous teachers. For those who have not been so fortunate, perhaps the following pages will help to introduce them to a new adventure which is as close as the nearest pet shop or even the back yard.

Myriad are the stories of animal loyalty and devotion. We marvel that so often animals display qualities that we despair of finding in sufficient quantity in the human species. Such feelings are not entirely justified, of course, for humans have soared to some tremendous heights of being and achievement. But we are bewildered that man, capable of climbing the highest mountains, can also plunge into the most dismal of abysses. In those moments of contemplating man's state and destiny upon this globe, we sometimes imagine that only he has the ability to understand what life is all about. And the animal, on the other hand, is not plagued by doubts and imponderable questions. He is a loving, trusting, innocent child of nature who can be expected to behave in a specific manner under a certain set of conditions.

And then one day we discover that in many ways our babe in the woods is much more aware than we are of the universe in which we all live. He is less locked into a world bounded by the five senses than the general run of mankind. He is more sensitive to psychic phenomena, the presence of apparitions, disembodied spirits; he can monitor happenings hundreds of miles away, has greater precognition of homecomings, tragedies, and natural and manmade calamities, and can locate a target several thousand miles distant without a trail or clue or any previous acquaintance with the route.

We imagine that animals other than ourselves are simple creatures. How, then, do we explain that a dog will kill a cat and another dog will go to great lengths to save the life of one? How do we explain why some animals will spend months, even years, seeking a lost master, and another creature of the same species cares not at all who feeds him as long as the amount is sufficient? How do we explain how a pet can know of his owner's death in another country and another pet doesn't appear to be aware even if it's happening in the next room? How would we explain the behavior of a German shepherd racing across town to protect his mistress, knowing she will be in danger, when another shepherd is oblivious from the next room?

The parallels that can be drawn are endless and the discrepancies enormous. One eventually has to assume that animals, even dogs of the same breed, are as different as people.

Those who claim to understand dogs, let them explain if they can the talents of Missie, the clairvoyant Boston terrier; the basset who protects rabbits; the dogs who came back from the dead to warn their former masters of danger; Dox, who not only trailed criminals but pieced together evidence; Duke, who chose political sides; Chips, who risked his neck to save his company from machinegun fire; Strongheart, who taught meditation; the phantom dog who protected a stranger from assault; Mr. Lucky and Blitz, who spoke human language; and the many, many other cases of something other than expected canine behavior.

Those who know all there is to know about cats are challenged to explain Timothy, who repented of his crimes; Gypsy, who understood the difference between standard and daylight savings time; cats who prophesy death; Willy, who always knew when it was Bingo night; the cat who always showed for Thursday auctions but never at other times; the cats who minimized human deaths during the London blitz by means of precognition; cats who send telepathic messages; the cat who chose to remain on his master's grave; the ghost cat of Congleton.

Many experienced horse breeders and trainers might have some difficulty explaining how the wildest and meanest of steeds would obey John Solomon Rorey within minutes; the talking horses of Elberfeld; Lady Wonder, the telepathic horse; the ghost horse of the White Mountains; the phantom horses of Colorado; the horses who have refused to be given away; and the supersenses of a horse who saved a group of sick people from freezing to death.

How might any of us explain the canary who died so her mistress could live; beavers who blanketed themselves around a lost boy to keep him from freezing; the baboon who cared and worked for his crippled master; the cow who volunteered for seeing-eye duties; the bees who attended their keeper's funeral; bears who understand herbal remedies; crabs who monitor ocean tides a thousand miles from the sea; swans who traditionally fly a strange flight formation as a requiem for their dying masters; the personalized language of ravens; the cosmic clocks of migratory birds? We are taxed even further to explain the sheer genius and saintly qualities of the dolphin, the intellectual of the sea with a larger and more complex brain than our own. He challenges the very pedestal on which man proclaims his superiority.

J. Allen Boone was told by an old desert recluse that if he wanted to understand a dog, he should ask the dog. The American Indians did just that, and so today do Fred Kimball and Beatrice Lydecker, who talk to animals, and Mildred Probert's dialogue with Missie challenges us to go "to the horse's mouth." People can only give you opinions about animals, not answers, Desert Dan said.

On the following pages we hear from animals, and Indians, scientists, naturalists, psychics, trainers, and pet lovers throughout the world. Stories are told, cases cited, experiments revealed, and theories proposed.

I hope this book will encourage you to join me in my admiration and awe for the creatures large and small who are sharing this earth trip with us. The better we understand one of these fellow citizens the better we understand ourselves. Finally, this is an adventure in consciousness, lately referred to as the only game in town.

1

New Maps of Consciousness

He was advised to treat him as an intelligent human being, never to say anything to him with his lips that he did not mean in his heart, and to read something worthwhile to him every day.

Strange instruction, thought J. Allen Boone, writer, producer, and one-time head of RKO movie studios, for someone caring for a dog. Not an ordinary dog, certainly, for this was Strongheart, international champion German shepherd and famous movie celebrity. Nevertheless, Boone was not prepared for the lessons he was to learn from his four-footed companion.

Shortly after Strongheart arrived at Boone's home, a conflict of lifestyles ensued, and Boone complained to the dog. Strongheart listened attentively and then proceeded through pantomime to illustrate in some detail the reasons for his behavior.

"I had spoken to Strongheart in my kind of language, a language of thoughts and feelings incased in human sound symbols," Boone stated in *Kinship with All Life*. "He had actually been able to receive and understand what I had said. Then he had answered me in his kind of language, a language made up of simple sounds and pantomime which he obviously felt I could follow without too much difficulty. Strongheart had understood me perfectly, and then with his keen and penetrating dog wisdom he had made it possible for me to understand him, too.

"For the first time, I was actually conscious of being in rational correspondence with an animal. With the dog's patient and guiding help, we have been able to communicate our individual states of mind to each other, to exchange points of view and thereby to solve a difficulty that threatened to mar our relationship. His innate wisdom had topped my intellectual reasoning at every point. I realized how little I knew about the mental capacities of a dog and his ability to express those capacities in a practical way.

"I had been privileged to watch an animal, acting upon its own initiative, put into expression qualities of independent thinking . . . of clear reasoning . . . of good judgment . . . of foresight . . . of prudence . . . of common sense. I had been taught to believe these qualities belonged more or less exclusively to the members of the human species, or rather to the 'educated members' of our species. And here was a dog overflowing with them!"

Every animal lover has stories to tell about the unusual mental powers of dogs and cats and a host of other creatures great and small, and most will have at least one story of unexplainable psychic powers of animals. An infallible ice-breaker in almost any crowd is an anecdote of a dog who did something he couldn't do.

Such tales fascinate young and old alike. Why is this so? The storyteller believes his story, and we have little reason to question its truth. Yet, there is something of the romanticist in most of us that restrains us from turning the spinning of animal yarns into a scientific probe. Perhaps we love a mystery and find a world resplendent with unknowns somehow more intriguing than one reduced to formulas.

But the moments of questioning remain; while man is entertained by the unknown, his rational mind nevertheless seeks to explain it.

And what happens when we peek behind the skull of

the animal, when we divide it into little pieces? Can human and animal intelligence be meaningfully compared?

In order to determine the level of human intelligence, we measure a series of abilities. As different intelligence tests measure different abilities, the tests are impossible to compare. Because of this problem, human intelligence tests cannot be directly applied to other animals. Other animals live under different circumstances and therefore use quite different abilities.

These differences are pointed out by Vincent and Margaret Gaddis in their book *The Strange World of Animals and Pets*: "Many wild animals become pathetic neurotics in captivity. In zoos they are deprived of the environments they require for normal behavior. They often react to monotony and frustration with violence; others suffer chronic depressions, sexual obsessions or inhibitions, and emotional ills that cause physical damage and even death.

"To attempt to make intelligence tests of wild creatures after they are imprisoned and their behavior patterns shattered, their senses torpid, and their minds sluggish, is ridiculous. Only in their natural habitat does their natural brilliance shine forth."

The authors quote Ralph Helfer, Hollywood animal trainer, as saying that it is a mistake to believe that animals think in the same way that humans do. "People mistakenly rate the intelligence of animals by their own," Helfer said. "There is a wild intelligence in a tiger that is top rate, but which is different from our thinking."

"Laboratory experimenters seeking to determine animal intelligence use mazes or puzzle boxes, or have their subjects push or peck the right symbol to obtain a food reward," the Gaddises continue. "These methods and similar ones are unsatisfactory, and at best may rate only the intelligence level and response time of the individual subject. For not only do the levels between various species vary, but there can be great differences between individuals within each species. There are smart cats and there are stupid cats. This explains why zoologists cannot agree on a specific intelligence scale."

The higher the intelligence of an animal the less he is guided by instinct and the more he must learn from his parents. To a large extent he must be prepared to solve problems on his own. Such higher animals require a considerable period of time for learning and maturation. While it has been held that the human has the longest maturation period of any animal as regards mental faculties, it seems that the elephant takes equally long. Domesticated elephants are not considered mature enough to work until they are about twenty years old. And some believe that it takes the sperm whale longer than the human and elephant to mature.

In *Smarter Than Man?* Swedish authors Karl-Erik Fichtelius and Sverre Sjolander define intelligence as ". . . the ability to differentiate, to combine and generalize, to analyze and associate, to perceive continuity and arrive at the concept of cause and effect, to imagine the results of contemplated actions, to deliberate and find the means of reaching a desired goal."

As an example of this kind of intelligence, Fichtelius and Sjolander tell of two dolphins playing with an eel. The eel eluded them by diving into a hole in the bottom. But one of the dolphins seized a small fish with a poison sting, took it carefully in its mouth, and pushed it in the hole where the eel was hiding. The eel immediately fled from the hole, and so the game continued. The episode was reported by the well-known Danish ethologist Holger Poulsen.

"Dolphins can learn by observation," Fichtelius and Sjolander explain. "In the shows given at aquariums it often happens that the dolphin expected to perform a certain trick fails to do so for some reason. It has been reported on several occasions that dolphins completely untrained for this trick have stepped in and performed it perfectly. This kind of learning by observation has otherwise been reported only in human beings and apes."

In *Elephant* by J. H. Williams, the story is told of an elephant that was being used to lift large logs very high. It was necessary for the animal to balance the logs at right angles on the upper side of its trunk. Several logs had fallen into positions that made it extremely dangerous for the driver if they fell from the height at which they were perched. Without instruction of any kind, the elephant dropped the log it was holding and grabbed a heavy beam lying nearby and placed it vertically between its trunk and one tusk. It then lifted the log while the beam stood there as a barrier protecting the driver.

Williams also tells how two young elephants stuffed mud into the bells hanging about their necks and thus prevented them from ringing. They then proceeded to steal bananas quietly during the night and managed to plunder entire banana groves undetected.

It is difficult to measure how intelligent dolphins and elephants are because we have not yet determined what their large brains are used for. Evidently, these animals have found their brains useful; they serve a purpose beyond our ability to understand. The human appears to be the most intelligent of the animals according to our intelligence tests, but we are not necessarily the most intelligent if this means the capacity to alter behavior in response to changing information from the environment, according to Fichtelius and Sjolander.

The fascinating case of the dolphin will be discussed later, but we can justifiably state here that a great deal more needs to be learned about brains in general before any final conclusions can be drawn.

Many scientists are now speculating that brain and mind are not synonymous. Here they find themselves in agreement with mystics who have long claimed that the organic brain cannot be the sole component of mentality, that there is a nonphysical mind which uses the physical brain as an instrument. Within this model, the mind is not dependent on the brain for its existence. Actually, they say, the reverse is true: the mind creates and uses the brain in order to function within a physical body. If this model is accurate, the examination of the brain will fail to yield the nature, source, and degree of intelligence. The complexity of the brain—when fully understood—may provide us with some measure of insight as to how this control center operates a body capable of many activities.

Where all of this seems to be taking us is toward a conception of consciousness as not something produced by a body, nervous system, and brain but the other way around. A certain expression of consciousness creates a certain body, nervous system, and brain. We might venture that a particular kind of body system can contain or be the expression of a particular type of consciousness. However, it would seem that a study of the body system would provide us with an understanding of the nature of its consciousness only if we understand all of its various expressions. At this point we are still mapping and exploring our own consciousness, and it seems likely that our understanding of awareness other than our own is even less complete.

There is some evidence that part of the mind is in touch with every thing in the universe, ignoring form, space, and time. Solving the riddles as to the nature of man and the other animals upon this planet may depend less on bisecting gray matter and mental guessing games and more on understanding the unified consciousness in which all life forms move and have their being.

"There is life on earth—one life, which embraces every animal and plant on the planet. Time has divided it up into several million parts, but each is an integral part of the whole. A rose is a rose, but it is also a robin and a rabbit. We are all of one flesh, drawn from the same crucible," biologist Lyall Watson tells us in *Supernature*. "This is the secret of life. It means that there is a continuous communication not only between living things and their environment, but among all things living in that environment. An intricate web of interaction connects all life into one vast, self-maintaining system. Each part is related to every other part and we are all part of the whole . . ."

Each part is related to every other part . . . how else can we explain how a bond could be so close between a man and his dog that the dog, with the instinct to survive, nevertheless gives up his life to save his master? Into what wavelength was Bobbie tuned in that it would direct her over three thousand unknown miles to find her family?

Vincent and Margaret Gaddis relate a story told by the naturalist Alan Devoe of a man named Phil Traband who was hiking in the woods. He heard sounds behind him and turned to see a large cat, a lynx, coming toward him. The lynx is generally considered mean and dangerous, but Traband held his ground and waited. ''As the big cat drew near, he could see in her eyes the unmistakable look of a kindred spirit appealing for help. The cat's mouth and muzzle were swollen, and as the man—almost instinctively—reached out a hand, the animal opened her mouth. In some manner one of the lynx's fangs had pierced the tongue and held it fast. The wound had become infected.

''A groan of pain rumbled in the cat's throat as Traband held her mouth open and, as lightly as he could, worked the swollen tongue free from the impaling fang. The act required several long minutes and must have been very painful, but the wildcat stood quietly. When the tongue was free, the still-incredulous man patted the tawny back. A glow of thankfulness appeared in the cat's eyes and with a soft 'mrroww,' the lynx slipped away into the woods.''

How are we to understand this story? How did the big cat know that understanding and help would be found in the man she followed? On some level there was communication, some depth of meaning forever eluding the test tube and scalpel.

2

They Talk to Animals

"You have a fat little dog there."

"Yes," I replied without hesitation; there is no other way to describe our overfed female basset. "She's fat all right, and her name is Sady."

"Well, let's see what Sady has to say about the state of affairs . . ." There was a pause and then, "Sady says she doesn't do a lot, just sits and watches but doesn't miss much."

How very true. We have never had a pet that is as observant as our five-year-old woeful-eyed basset. While she doesn't chase around the farm a great deal, she always seems to be near enough to the action to be taking it all silently in. You can look up from what you're doing and Sady is watching, often placing herself in such a position that she can observe various fields of activity.

"Sady says you have a limp and she seems worried about that."

"No, I . . ." but I paused in my first impulse to deny such an affliction, remembering that I had stepped on a rusty nail several days before and was still favoring the foot.

"She also says that there is an older man there who has trouble with his neck."

"This would refer to my father, who lives next door, and has been having trouble with pain and stiffness in his neck for a couple of years now."

"There is a woman there whom she loves and who loves her but who gets cranky sometimes when she tracks in mud or steals something sweet off the kitchen table. She says this woman talks a lot but she sure can't sing."

"Well, she certainy pegged me," my wife said laughingly later. "That blabbermouth!"

As for tracking in dirt and mud, Sady is guilty of that, and there is nothing she is more adept at than stealing cake, cookies, and candy left unattended on a table.

Serving as an interpreter for our pet was Fred Kimball, known as "the man who talks to animals." He is an accomplished psychic and clairvoyant. How do we know, then, that he wasn't simply reading my mind? Perhaps it isn't *a priori* evidence, but Sady also told Kimball a couple of things that I had no way of knowing until I later confirmed them: She had stashed a certain toy in a corner of her doghouse and she had hidden a bone in a spot I was able to locate.

There is something very smug and bigoted about human nature. It has the habit of assuming that *Homo sapiens* is the only creature with any real kind of intelligence. We have come to accept mindreading and telepathic exchange between people, but eyebrows usually raise when you hint that a two-footed creature and a four-footed one have been carrying on a conversation. For some odd reason we find it easier to accept the idea that animals can read our minds than the reverse. It is not at all unusual for a pet lover to tell how his dog always knows ahead of time that he is planning a hike in the woods or is planning to leave town for a few days. We marvel at these abilities, accept them as being real enough, and yet, without noticing our contradictions, are not willing to allow the animal sufficient equipment to perform these acts.

In any case, Fred Kimball has been behaving for many years as though animals have minds, and this acceptance has provided him with some lively dialogues with all kinds of furry and feathered conversants in many parts of the world. He tunes in on animals' thoughts, lets them know he would like to converse with them, and if they do—sometimes they don't—they will tell him about their lives, their likes and dislikes, about the people and other animals in their lives. Sometimes they voice complaints or register some request with Kimball.

A horse was being treated for lameness in its hindquarters. The condition was getting worse despite the efforts of several excellent veterinarians. In desperation, the owners asked Kimball to ask the horse what was wrong with him.

"I backed into a rough board in my stable and drove a splinter into my spinal column," the horse informed the psychic. This information was referred to a veterinarian, and close examination revealed this to be the case. The splinter was removed and the horse got well.

One might say that Kimball is a pet consultant. A lot of people talk to their animals, but Kimball listens to them when they answer. He is a nationally known psychic who has appeared on network television and radio shows and has been interviewed by many newspapers, and he lectures widely in this and other countries. He is approached by pet owners and trainers and consults with veterinarians about difficult animal patients. He maintains two California homes, one in Gardena and a retreat place in Idyllwild.

So what else is odd about Fred Kimball? Has he lived in a cave or a treehouse most of his life learning to howl and to warble? No, it hasn't been necessary for him to live with animals in the wild or endeavor to imitate their sounds. His communication is on the level of mental images; verbal exchange is not necessary.

Actually, in many ways, Kimball is a man of the world,

one who has lived an active and colorful life. At one time or another he has been a professional boxer, wrestler, champion swimmer, rifle instructor for the army, counselor, coach in the Marine Corps, judo expert, steel processor, and hypnotist. A large, vigorous man, he appears to be in his fifties instead of his early seventies. For more than fifty years he has been involved in psychic research, to which he now devotes full time as an ordained minister, and he continues to counsel and lecture. Of the many paths trod by Kimball one of the most profitable has been sailing the earth's seas as a merchant marine. His travels allowed him the opportunity to study the teachings of many cultures, including Oriental systems of body and mind control.

Curiously, Kimball was not psychic as a child. As a Massachusetts farm boy, part of his chores was to milk the cows. "Nothing is worse," he said, "than the swipe of a wet cow's tail across your face at four a.m. I got so I hated cows." At age nine he became interested in hypnotism and for a time performed as a carnival hypnotist. He gave up hypnotism as a practice when he was thirty-nine, but gives it some credit for helping him to develop his psychic powers.

But he was past forty when he first understood what animals were saying. He was standing sentinel on the deck of a tanker and was watching the flight of a seagull as it glided across the bow of the ship. The graceful bird soared skyward, then reversed its flight and winged its way starboard. As it glided closer to the sailor, it called out, "Hi, Fred!"

"I thought I had been at sea too long when that happened," he said with a craggy grin. "At first I was sure someone had called my name. I looked around. No one was there. The greeting came again. Surely someone was calling to me. Again I looked around but I was alone, and as the graceful bird soared above me I began to realize I was picking up the seagull's thought waves."

Kimball worked for a time with the late Dr. Nandor Fodor, one of New York's foremost psychiatrists and an early researcher in extrasensory perception. It was during this period that he experienced his first two-way communication with an animal. Between sessions with Dr. Fodor, he spent a lot of time observing the animals at the Central Park Zoo, studying their habits and movements. One day he was watching a lion. The animal kept pacing his cage in a very animated fashion and Kimball sensed that something was wrong.

"I tried putting myself in tune with his thought waves and I asked him what he was thinking about.

" 'Sex!' the lion replied.

"I went to the caretaker and I asked the man why his lion was so obsessed with sex. 'He should be,' the caretaker replied, 'the lioness in the next cage is in heat.' "

Communicating with animals is not easy, according to Kimball, as they have very limited vocabularies. They communicate through images. They send a picture that Kimball sees in his mind and interprets. The modern-day Dr. Doolittle voices his questions simply and holds a mental vision of what he is saying at the same time. The animal flashes back a mind picture and Kimball translates it and relays the information to the pet's owner, trainer, or whoever is involved. At times, he gets the distinct impression of words. Explaining this, he said, "If you were to see a horrible car accident, blood and bodies all about, you might say something to the effect, 'That's terrible' or 'That's horrible.' In other words I get a distinct emotional impression that can easily be translated into a simple vocabulary."

His mind has become so adapted to animals, he notes, that a fellow psychic tuned in on his mind once and commented, "For a minute I got mixed up. I thought it was a dog talking."

Recently a woman called Kimball and asked if he would "read" her pet dog, who had suddenly taken to soiling the rug. The dog told Kimball that the woman had just gotten a divorce. The dog loved the man and felt the divorce was the woman's fault. He told Fred, "She evacuated him and I am evacuating on the rug.'' The dog added that he hated the woman and did not want to be with her any longer.

Kimball questioned the woman and asked her if she had recently become divorced. Somewhat startled, she answered that she had. He related the dog's message and suggested that she find the pet another home as he had no intention of changing his behavior.

He once interviewed Mae West's monkeys. One of them told him about a visitor who had watched them playing, and he said gleefully, ''I turned the water on him.'' The psychic assumed that the monkey meant he had turned a water hose on the visitor. But Miss West explained that the monkey had hooked his tail about a pail of water standing nearby, drawn it into the cage, and then thrown the whole thing into the face of her chagrined visitor.

''You see,'' Kimball explained, ''the monkey's vocabulary didn't include the word 'pail' or the idea of 'pail,' so he expressed himself as saying he turned the water on the fellow.''

Kimball's paranormal abilities are not limited to animals; a great deal of his time is spent doing readings and counseling people. As with other clairvoyants, he sees the aura surrounding and permeating the body; can perceive significant portions of a person's past, present, and future; can learn intimate details of a person's life by handling a photograph of him or letter written by him; can see the interior of the human body; can make an accurate diagnosis of physical and mental problems and offer constructive therapeutic suggestions.

In *Many Lives, Many Loves*, author Dr. Gina Cerminara tells of inviting Kimball to her home one evening, along with sixteen other guests. She had never met Kimball before, nor did he know any of the guests. Several brought their pets for readings, and the animals were kept in their cars until their turns.

He first tried to talk to a German shepherd, part husky, named Jack, according to Dr. Cerminara. Jack was too excited because of the crowd, wouldn't settle down, and the only thing that Kimball was able to get from the dog was that he would die in six months. Later this was verified by the owners.

Duchess, also a German shepherd, told the psychic that she enjoyed riding in the family's white station wagon and sticking her nose out the window on the left side of the front seat, resting her head on the driver's neck. She had a close attachment to the husband but thought the children were nuisances. All of the details were confirmed by the owners.

A small mongrel dog told all about himself, where he lived and about his surroundings, and then he mentioned that he liked to sleep on a leather-covered couch in a room next to the bathroom. However, a little girl that lived in the home would go into the bathroom whenever she got upset, sit underneath the water basin, and cry her heart out. The dog said he became very unhappy whenever this happened. Quite amazed, the owner of the dog stated that this was true.

The session in Dr. Cerminara's home included talks with a French poodle that felt neglected and unloved and a cat that caught most of the lectures at the Theosophical Society Lodge next door to where it lived. Apparently it was quite a successful evening and the psychologist was to write of Kimball in her book:

"It is significant, first of all, because it demonstrates a new extension in the range of clairvoyance. Clairvoyance has been directed at many targets of interest, and undoubtedly other gifted people have looked into the minds and bodies of animals. But seldom, if ever, does one hear of it; and if one does, it is seldom, if ever, accompanied by the evidential details whereby its veracity can be at least partially confirmed.

Kimball's work is deserving, therefore, I feel, of extended study, and what he does should commend itself to other sensitives, for their own exploration . . .

"But Kimball's work has been of interest to me principally because it points, I think, to something of great significance as regards the inner world of animals. Any cat lover or dog lover would find it valuable to know something of what our four-footed friends cannot convey to us through speech. But apart from this immediate and personal satisfaction, there is a broader and deeper implication. Kimball's capacity shows us dramatically that where there is life there is mind and consciousness; that animals are endowed with a sensitive psychological awareness comparable to our own; and that behind their alert bright eyes lies an acute faculty for judgment and appraisal that we ordinarily do not think about because it does not manifest itself in human speech.''

An interesting experience occurred to Kimball several years ago in Silver City, New Mexico, at the St. John's Mine. While waiting for a friend who worked at the mine, Kimball sat down on a cable spool. He soon noticed a large, golden-haired dog coming toward him with a great deal of red in the aura about his head, and the psychic recognized this as indicative of an affliction about the head. He patted him and commented, ''You must be a good fighter.'' The dog said that he had been, then he turned and disappeared into a nearby tunnel. A few seconds later Kimball heard a short bark, and he had a mental picture of the dog tumbling headlong down a shaft, striking his head on something at the bottom and lying still.

Kimball quickly fetched the mine foreman. They found the dog had entered a newly opened section of the mine and had fallen down a forty-five-foot shaft. The foreman stated that the dog was blind (explaining the red aura) and relied on his sense of smell to get around. As this was a new section of the mine the dog had no way of knowing about the open shaft.

The miners were able to lift the unconscious dog from the shaft and decided that it would be more merciful to shoot him. Kimball, however, was able to tune in mentally with the animal, and he asked, ''Are you going to die?'' The reply came back, ''Not unless you kill me.'' Kimball told the message to the miners and their decision was to try to nurse him back to health. In no time at all he recovered.

Kimball believes that the most intelligent and fearless canines are the German shepherds. "These large animals feel they can kill anything and they aren't afraid of anyone. Actually, intelligence is not the exclusive property of any breed or species, but for some reason or other I have run in to more intelligent German shepherds than any other kind of dog. The little dogs are the insecure ones and they often tell me, 'I risk my life every time I go outside.' " He feels that this fear may have a great deal to do with the nervous temperament of small dogs.

The manner in which he determines the true intelligence of an animal is its ability to create vivid mental pictures. Kimball does not agree with the commonly held belief that dogs are colorblind. "Intelligent dogs convey colors quite easily," he states. "Animals of lesser intelligence are not as aware of colors."

Cats are secretive and likely to be less communicative than dogs, Kimball claims. One of the most intelligent creatures he ever talked with was a fourteen-year-old duck by the name of Mrs. Quacker. The duck described her owner's health problems in some detail. The diagnosis was confirmed by the man's wife.

Animals do not normally have large vocabularies, according to Kimball. For example, one dog told him that she enjoyed chasing "stinking cats," which was her way of describing skunks.

"Animals reflect to a large extent what they see in the people around them," the clairvoyant explained. "During one demonstration that I gave in Hollywood I could barely hear a hamster. I asked him why he was talking so low and the little creature said, 'The old woman in the house won't let anyone talk very loud. She doesn't like noises.' I discovered that the old woman referred to was the grandmother of the family. She was in the audience and quite taken aback that the hamster had the nerve to confront her in that mannner but she did admit it was true.''

A seven-year-old cocker spaniel named Gypsy told Kimball that she had come to the session in a new dark-green car. She described her house and listed the members of the family by name. She was confused, though, when describing one of the boy's girl friends. Gypsy thought she lived at the house because she saw the girl opening the refrigerator door a great deal. She also told the psychic that her leg had been broken and that it had been patched with permanent wires. Kimball found this to be interesting because the dog did not even limp.

Kimball once summoned a gopher out of its hole twice in Harmony Park to feed it, but when a curious youngster got too close, the animal excused itself, saying, ''I don't trust that boy,'' and he disappeared into his hole.

Snakes, leopards, eagles, pigs, lizards, and tigers have sent out their vibrations to the man who can understand them. He even tuned in on a can of earthworms at one time. ''They said they had come from the right side of the building and that there were five of them in the can. A count proved this to be the case.''

On a recent visit to the mountains, he encountered a mounted deer's head. He had the impression that the deer smiled at him and so he concentrated on it. ''At first I was saddened that the poor animal had been shot, but then I conjured up a picture of the Donner party which had been lost in the high country. Once I generated a rapport with the deer, I learned that the animal had been shot to provide meat for a group of starving people who were living in an old mining tunnel in the Colorado Rockies. The deer indicated that it was not saddened because of the way it had given its life.''

After talking to the entries of a horse race, Kimball picked fourteen of seventeen winners. Fortunately for the tracks, however, he does not take advantage of his unusual talents.

While he prefers to be in personal contact with animals, Kimball can communicate with animals, as well as people, through ESP. He exercises this side of his talent when people call him long distance for readings on their pets, usually involving some health problem or cases where the pets are lost. In the latter instance, he tries to tune in on the animal and when in contact asks the lost animal to describe what it can about its surroundings. Through this method he is sometimes able to identify the location well enough so that the animal can be found.

While talking about Fred Kimball to a friend I elicited the response, "He sounds as though he is quite accomplished, but he isn't the only one who talks to animals."

"Oh, I know," I replied. "We all do to some extent, I suppose, perhaps mostly unconsciously, and I'm sure there are many people that we never hear about who are able to communicate with all forms of life. Castaneda experienced this in his association with Don Juan, and there are shamans, yogis, not to mention the American Indian, who supposedly can tune their minds to any other mind—be it an insect or an elephant—in the universe."

"Yes," my friend responded, "but I mean there is another well-known personality who does much the same thing as Kimball. She is a woman and has been on the Mike Douglas Show several times."

He didn't know her name, but I figured Kimball would. He did. "Sure, that's Beatrice Lydecker, a good friend of mine. You really should visit with her. She really does a fine job of communicating with animals."

At this writing I've yet to meet Miss Lydecker. She is in great demand as a counselor and speaker, and with my traveling we have been something like ships passing in the night. But I've talked with her on the phone and she was kind enough to send me quite a lot of material on herself—background, newspaper clippings, letters, talk announcements, and so on. After reading this information, I am determined to meet her, and Sady, our basset, has indicated a similar interest: she carried off one of the clippings and was reluctant about releasing it.

When Miss Lydecker was small she didn't dream of growing up and becoming a translator of animal language. Actually, she had planned on becoming a missionary to orphaned children and is a graduate of a bible college. Then one day seven years ago while teaching in Duarte, California, her attention was drawn to a large German shepherd locked in a yard and she experienced the sensation that the animal was endeavoring to communicate with her. She approached the dog and suddenly knew what he was thinking and feeling. He told her he was sad because he was left alone so much of the time. She located the owner and learned that he had been injured some months before and had bought the dog for company. When he became well enough to work again, the dog was left alone during the day.

Messages from animals continued to come through to her. The unexpected nature of these experiences troubled her, and she shared her misgivings with her interdenominational prayer group. They felt that it was a gift from God and encouraged her to follow the gift wherever it might lead.

It led her in one instance to a Doberman who was being used as a guard dog at a large used-car lot. He had established a reputation in the neighborhood as a vicious beast. She passed this corner several times and on each occasion she distinctly heard someone calling her name. It also seemed to her to be a call for help. She would look around, but only the dog would be in sight. Finally, she realized that it was the Doberman who was calling out to her. She approached him and he allowed her to pat him; she recalls the strange looks she received from passersby, for even as she stroked his head and back the dog was snarling at people on the other side of the fence.

Loneliness had led him to call out to her, he said. He was desperate for loving attention and despised his image as a dangerous creature which resulted in his alienation from people.

And the gift led her to confide in a few friends, who

confided in a few other friends, and the young woman soon found herself consulting on all kinds of pets. She went back to school to study anatomy, chemistry, zoology, and psychology. In the years since she has communicated with many members of the animal kingdom, from lizards to leopards.

Her experiences with animals opened the way for an important contribution to the human species. She is now communicating with nonverbal persons—the severely retarded, autistic children, stroke victims, cerebral palsy sufferers. She spent a recent summer at a California Institute for the autistic and retarded.

The Glendale, California, psychic recalled a two-year-old child who had never acknowledged the existence of any other living being. Shut off from the world, he had responded to nothing that was done for him. But she communicated. She found the child was suffering from severe emotional and physical trauma caused at birth and wanted to return to the security and comfort of the womb. The only thing he seemed to enjoy was being rocked.

Miss Lydecker discovered—and later had the information comfirmed by the doctors—that the infant had been born to a thirteen-year-old girl who did not want the baby and who had a difficult time delivering. The staff started rocking the baby, and before Miss Lydecker left the institute the child had started crawling toward a person who was coming to rock him. This was viewed as quite a breakthrough.

"Everything alive communicates basically in the same manner," she told me. "It is subjective communication, which we all have as children but as we grow up and start to use language we tend to lose this quality. Subjective communication allows you to say what you really feel."

Miss Lydecker describes this type of communication somewhat like a dream, "only the person is wide awake. Mental pictures come through in which one sees, hears, tastes, and experiences life.

"Any animal can read your mind," she states. "The thought is in pictures and this is what the pets see; for this reason a person who thinks he may get bitten by a dog stands a pretty good chance of having his mental image fulfilled. Pets also see images of owners even when those images are not directly related to the pet." She told how a German shepherd had taken up the habit of tearing up tissue. The shepherd's master had died and the psychic learned that the dog was trying to share its mistress's grief.

Distance, it seems, has little bearing on the communication between people and their pets. According to Miss Lydecker, the animals will receive images from their owners who may be thousands of miles away, knowing, for example, when their owners are in danger or preparing to return home. For this reason, she says, pet owners who place their pets in kennels while they are on vacation and then worry about them the entire time shouldn't be too surprised to return home and find the pets have been ill or haven't been eating.

Miss Lydecker, referred to on occasion as the touring animal analyst, travels the country in a van with three German shepherds, Princess, Lover Boy, Philea, a Pomeranian, Blackie, and two cats, Tigger and Snow Bunny. Crowded into her busy schedule is work on a doctor's degree and a book, *What the Animals Tell Me*.

She has casual chats as well as deep conversations with animals. Her little thirteen-year-old Pomeranian told her he had been lost in Las Vegas by his owner—Julie or Judy, but she isn't sure—but that it was all right for her to keep him as he had not been with his previous owner long enough for her to be too attached.

Animals, like people, aren't always in a conversational mood. One day her German shepherd, Princess, was staring wistfully out the window. Assuming that something important was on the dog's mind, she started to tune in, but in a few seconds Princess looked toward her and distinctly told her to mind her own business. Roy

Roger's horse, Trigger, Jr., took one look at her and turned away.

But the calves at the rodeo told her they enjoyed the rough-and-tumble life of the rodeo, although they couldn't stand the guy with the "hot stick," evidently referring to the man with the electric probe used for prompting the calves to jump into the arena.

The bucking horses at the rodeo said they would be bored with some other kind of life, but the great racing horse of a few years back, Secretariat, was not so happy with his fate. He told Miss Lydecker that he missed the company of his former groom, was lonely for the exciting activity of racing, and missed the sheer joy of running. He said he was bored with lazing around the pasture and being used as a stud. She explained that animals do not get much of an emotional thrill out of sex; for them, it's entirely physical.

Most pets are overfed and underexercised, much too pampered and often bored. "Owners are stubborn," Miss Lydecker explained. "I've counseled with owners of pets and discovered that the pets can't stand their owners. In these situations I try to suggest tactfully to the owner that perhaps the pet needs a new home. I remember one session when the owner kept repeating, 'But he's been with us for three years. The poor thing would never adjust to another home.' And all this time the dog was appealing to me, 'Get me away from these people.' "

She helps many owners to find lost pets and has been successful in locating animals even long distances from their homes. She tunes in and listens to the animal describe its surroundings, including houses, cars, and sometimes names. A fat scrapbook is kept to document this work, and it is filled with letters from pet owners expressing their gratitude, many of which state, "I still don't understand how you did it, but . . ."

And how would we understand how Fred Kimball and Beatrice Lydecker talk with animals? Is it really so strange, or is it that we have forgotten how to communicate with life and imagine that language is the only way? If our model of universal consciousness is a viable one, then all things large and small have their being within this Awareness; all forms of life are lungs through which the Eternal breathes.

3

Missie, the
Clairvoyant Terrier

Accurate prophecies of natural catastrophes, political races, moon landings, world events, and even the moment of birth and death—these were the accomplishments of a Denver psychic. In comparing the successes of various prophets in recent years, the London *Daily Mail* called her one of the best.

No small achievement for a clairvoyant, but what boggles our minds is that this particular seer was a dog . . . or was she? The story of Missie, a Boston terrier, is a strange one, not easily understood, impossible to forget.

We have to deal with Missie; however we might try to explain her talents, she cannot be ignored. Her case has been too well documented, too many times witnessed and recorded to shrug off as a tale constructed by deluded reporters. What makes it so difficult to analyze the highly unusual activities of Missie is that her behavior doesn't fit into our models of what a dog can and cannot do. It is generally accepted that dogs can be psychically aware in a way that humans no longer can. That dogs are so in tune with life they can make their way across a continent to locate a lost family, even keep in touch with their owners telepathically—we can struggle with these accomplishments and with only mild bewilderment adjust our model a bit and yet keep it together. But a four-legged creature that can see the future, even to predicting the hour of its own death, and had such extrasensory powers that it could run through a whole deck of cards without making a mistake—a feat no human can boast—somehow this leaves us a little breathless.

Knowing that I was writing a book on animals, James Grayson Bolen, publisher of *Psychic*, sent me a back issue—September-October, 1973—of the magazine. In it was an article by Gina Cerminara, Ph.D., "Missie, the Psychic Dog of Denver." Familiar with Dr. Cerminara's books, I started the article with enthusiasm. After a few paragraphs, I was a mite stunned. I decided to get some more coffee. By the end of the article, the traffic in my mind was a little congested; I was having difficulty sorting out concepts. I decided to sleep on it. The following day I reread the article and tried adding it up in my mind. I concluded that neither *Psychic* magazine nor Dr. Cerminara would present to the reader anything but the facts as received and as understood by them. This being the case, they either did not have all the facts and there was some other explanation than clairvoyancy for Missie's accomplishments, or this dog was forcing upon us a complete revaluation of intelligence and knowledge, even the nature of life itself. That night I called the dog's owner.

Miss Mildred Probert was charming, and we talked for quite some time. She was pleasant, intelligent, well informed, and quite down to earth. I think maybe I expected her to be otherwise. She discussed her pet's activities and unusual accomplishments in a rational but matter-of-fact way. I was impressed and more convinced that whatever Missie was, she was not to be lightly dismissed.

More calls followed and we exchanged several letters, and early in the spring of 1976 my wife, Jeann'e and I paid a visit on Miss Probert at her home in Denver. An old Victorian-style home, it was filled with antiques, many of which her grandfather had brought over from his castle in Denmark. We were greeted at the door by a Boston terrier—not Missie, for she has been dead for several years.

This dog's name was Sissie, a cousin of Missie's, and Miss Probert quickly informed us that Sissie was not in any way psychic. She was delightful, nonetheless, and psychic enough to know that we loved dogs.

Sitting on the large, comfortable overstuffed divan, with the mementoes of Missie—photos, clothes, toys, scrapbooks—strewn about us, we listened enchanted and amazed as the story of Missie unfolded. Miss Probert has told of her famous dog many times, to visitors, newspapers, and on radio and television, but there was not the slightest effort on her part to skip important details. She knows that she was blessed by a gift, one that changed her life and one that can have considerable significance for mankind. There was not the slightest pretense about our hostess. She was sincere and candid, and her great love for her departed companion was obvious and touching. She is writing a book on Missie. We left there that evening believing it would be an important one.

Even the way Missie came into her life was unusual. Miss Probert had been a floral designer for a number of years and for a time had been manager and part owner of a pet shop. Bad health, however, had forced her into retirement, but she took in animals that needed special care or boarded them when their owners were out of town. One day she was given a tiny newborn Boston terrier to care for. It was too small to be left in the litter. Its birth was odd. The mother had been delivered of three puppies by the veterinarian and all went well until midnight some hours later—when the mother dog went into convulsions of pain. She was taken to the hospital and operated on, and high near the ribcage the veterinarian located a tiny unit of flesh which he first thought to be some kind of unwanted growth, but it was found to be a puppy.

Missie never knew her mother or her brothers and sisters. She knew only her human mother during the early stages of her life and, strangely enough, never grew to care for other dogs, preferring the company of people. She was extremely small for a Boston terrier, and there was a startling difference between her and other members of her breed. Boston terriers have dark, almost black eyes, but Missie's eyes were a deep cobalt blue. A few breeds of dogs have light-blue eyes, but quite unlike Missie's.

Missie was nearly five years old before her psychic talents were discovered. Miss Probert, her mother, and Missie were out walking one day and they came upon an acquaintance with her small child in tow. They asked the youngster to tell them his age. When he didn't answer, the mother said that he was timid but that he was three. Miss Probert leaned over the child and said, ''Three. Say, 'three.' '' The child remained silent, but Missie suddenly barked three times. Everyone laughed and Miss Probert said, ''Okay, smarty, how old are you?'' Missie barked four times. More than a little surprised, Miss Probert asked, ''How old will you be next week?'' Five distinctive barks was the reply, which was correct.

''That was the beginning,'' Miss Probert told us. ''It really wasn't a matter of my training her, for she knew things that I didn't. It was just a matter of trying to find out what she knew. It seemed endless.'' They tested Missie with fingers, asking her how many were being held up, and it was soon discovered that she could add. When she was asked such questions as ''If I hold up four fingers and then five more, how many fingers will that be?'' back would come the immediate and accurate response.

Miss Probert doesn't know how Missie learned to cope with numbers. ''She developed her system entirely on her own. If a series of numbers were involved, such as a street address or telephone number, she would bark so many times for the first number, pause, bark out the second number, pause, and so on. She gave out a strange little muffled sound for 'zero.' ''

Missie's uncanniness with numbers included not only addition and subtraction, but the number of letters in a word or name. Her extrasensory powers were discovered when a stranger to both Missie and her owner asked the dog to tell him his address. She barked out the numbers without hesitation. Miss Probert found that she could ask Missie to tell her how many letters were in the first name of a person she herself didn't know. Missie would bark out the correct number and would follow this with the last name.

On one occasion Missie was asked to give the number of letters in a woman's first name. Missie barked four times for "Mary." "How many letters are there in 'Merry' as in 'Merry Christmas'?" Back came the five barks. "How many letters in 'marry' as when two people get married?" Five barks again. Missie was constantly being tested on the number of letters in words, and she could invariably give the correct answer. She could do this whether or not Miss Probert was in the room, and she was tested in five languages. It is not known how many languages she was adept in for she was tested in only five.

At parties, Missie could be relied on to tell people how many coins were in their purses or how many beans were in a sack. Usually those present did not know beforehand the number involved.

Dr. Cerminara tells in her article how during one party Missie was asked to give the number of spots on a playing card as it was held up. "He held the cards in such a way that the back of the cards faced the dog and the assembled company . . . This was the first time that Missie had ever seen a deck of playing cards, and yet she went through the entire deck without a mistake. Since nobody in the room saw the face of the cards until after Missie barked the response, at which time the experimenter showed the card to everyone, this would seem to preclude the possibility of telepathy and make it a clear-cut case of clairvoyance. (When she came to a Jack, Queen, or King, she whined; then she was asked, 'Is this a picture card?' She barked three times for yes. Is it a King? Queen? Jack? She would bark yes when he came to the correct one.)"

Missie figured out her way of answering yes and no. In addition to barking three times for yes and twice for no, she managed to sound out a distinguishable "uh-huh" for yes and "huh-uh" for no. For example, for yes she would say "uh-huh, woof, woof, woof!" She also shook her head up and down for yes and sideways for no.

The small dog had health problems all of her life, including epilepsy, yet she had a great determination to live. She enjoyed life so much and her great enthusiasm for everything that was going on around her was infectious. One time when she had to enter the hospital for an operation, I asked the doctor what ward she would be in. He said he didn't know but Missie barked five times. The doctor said he didn't think she would be in that ward, but Missie was right.

"She could give you the correct serial numbers on dollar bills and the day, month, and year people—friends or strangers—were born. A physician we met was very skeptical of Missie's powers; he just wasn't going to be convinced. I finally said to him, 'Well, Doctor, there is one number that neither Missie nor I know and that is your private home number.' 'Oh,' he said, 'I never give that to anyone.' 'Go ahead,' I said to Missie, 'and tell us the doctor's private number, but we don't wish to hurt him so don't give us the last figure.' When she did it, he just leaned back in his chair perplexed. On another occasion I asked a doubting newsman, 'What is your social security number?' 'I don't remember,' he said. 'What is this gentleman's social security number, Missie?' When she was right, he became a believer. You see, people looked for the gimmick and in the end found there wasn't any. I never knew how she could do these things and was as perplexed as anyone over her achievements."

The small terrier's first psychic prediction was made on October 15, 1964, just before the elections and when everyone was pondering the outcome of the presidential race. Mildred had carried Missie into a local store where the clerks always enjoyed asking the dog questions. By way of conversation, Mildred said to the owner of the store, "Well, how many weeks until the election?" But before he could answer Missie barked three times, which was correct. Taken somewhat aback, Mildred queried, "How many days until the election, Missie?" The correct nineteen barks followed.

At this point the owner said, "Ask her who will win

the presidency." "But how could she know that?" Mildred objected. Several people in the store had gathered around Mildred and her dog and they insisted that she ask Missie the question. "If Mr. Johnson is one and Senator Goldwater is two, who will win the election?" Mildred asked. One bark followed. Mildred reversed the question: "If Barry Goldwater is one and Lyndon Johnson is two, who will win the election?" Missie barked twice.

Someone present at this gathering phoned the *Rocky Mountain News*. A reporter and photographer were sent out and on November 8, 1964, a picture appeared in the paper of Missie along with her prediction.

Many political predictions were to follow, but the only question she ever refused to answer was whether Johnson would seek a second term. "She just pushed out her little mouth and refused to answer," Mildred said. She predicted that Nixon would win the presidency, and she prophesied the outcome of many state and national political races, several that appeared very unlikely at the time.

Missie predicted the number of delays in the launching of Gemini 12, space probes, moon landings, and UFO sightings. On New Year's Eve of 1965 she was interviewed on KTLN, a Denver radio station, and after correctly barking the number of letters in "Happy New Year," she was asked, "When will the New York transit strike end?" She barked out January 13, and this proved to be correct. There had been some concern in the Denver area about an earthquake and Missie was asked if it was caused by natural phenomena. She answered no, and when asked when the real cause would be known, she said that it would be June. Sure enough, during that month it was learned that the cause of the quake was the result of the army placing waste material from nerve gases into an old well and the resulting explosions were thought to be quakes.

The following day, January 1, 1966, the small terrier with the penetrating blue eyes was on another radio station and predicted nine months in advance the outcome of the World Series, the day the series would end, and the correct score.

Missie's knowledge of future events seemed as vast as the imagination of those asking the questions. She foretold in her own ineffable fashion the failure of the atom smashing plant to be located in Denver, the date for the initiation of the Paris Peace Talks and their outcome, and the return of the Colorado National Reserve from the Vietnam War.

A letter from Gary Robinson to Mildred but addressed "To Whom It May Concern" read:

"When I was a moderator on a radio talk show on station K.T.L.N. Denver, Colo., I had a phone call from Mildred Probert on 9/30/65 (the day my baby girl was born). Miss Probert told me her 'psychic dog,' a Boston terrier, had been barking out a 'yes' answer, when asked if my baby would be a girl.

"This call was made before the baby was born.

"She put the dog on the phone to bark out the hour of time it was then and the temperature (which I checked with a phone temperature call).

"Missie also gave the date, Miss Probert asking 'What month, date, year and the day of the week?' And how many letters in my name? All without error. It brought me a rush of calls when I remarked it was 'the first time I talked to a dog and it answered back.'

"After that Missie performed over the phone on my program seven or eight times. Giving scores for forthcoming football games and the World Series baseball games, correctly.

"On New Year's Eve 1966, she gave answers for events occurring each month for the next year. All turned out to be true."

In many instances, Missie predicted the date, sex, and weight of an unborn child, including the birth of a girl to the Queen of Greece. Mildred stated, and the story is also told by Dr. Cerminara, that on one of these occasions, September 10, 1965, a pregnant woman stopped to visit with Missie and Mildred as they sat on their front lawn. Mildred mentioned the dog's ability to give correct data as to births. "Well," the woman replied, "I know what to expect concerning mine. I've lost two babies while carrying them and I have an appointment for a Caesarean operation for October 6.''

"Will this lady have her baby on October 6?" Mildred asked Missie. No, the dog replied, whereupon the woman became quite upset, thinking that this meant the baby would die as her other babies had. Immediately Mildred asked if the baby would be alive and Missie barked three times for yes.

"In what month will the baby be born?"

"I already know that," the woman objected. "October."

"No," Missie barked and followed this with nine barks, meaning September. She then proceeded to bark twice, a pause, and then barked eight times for the 28th.

"A girl?" Mildred asked. "No" was the answer. "A boy?" and Missie barked three times.

Again the woman objected. "The doctor is quite certain it will be a girl."

But Mildred continued to pursue the details. "What time will the baby be born?" Missie barked nine times. "Nine o'clock in the morning?" "No," was the answer. "In the evening," and Missie said yes.

"I'm afraid that's quite impossible," the lady-in-waiting exclaimed. "The doctor isn't in the hospital at night and he has scheduled the operation for nine o'clock in the morning."

"How much will the baby weigh?" Seven barks.

"Well, I doubt it," the woman said. "My other babies only weighed five pounds."

After that she took her leave, thanking the woman and dog for their interest and stating that she was amazed at the dog's comprehension of the questions but she was quite sure the dog was wrong on all counts. Mildred asked that she call when the baby came.

On the night of September 28, Mildred received an excited call from the woman's husband. "My wife became quite ill this evening and had to be rushed to the hospital," he exclaimed. "Her doctor was out of town and so another doctor assisted. She gave natural birth to a baby boy at exactly nine p.m." "How much did the baby weigh?" Mildred asked. "Seven pounds and the baby's fine!"

Once accepting the incredulous fact that a dog can be clairvoyant, one is faced with the question as to why it could be more accurate even than its human counterparts. One can only speculate that the universal source of information flows to human and dog seers alike, but perhaps the human rational mind gets in its own way, distorting the information, whereas the dog just passes it along in whatever way it can. Was all of this vast knowledge of past, present, and future events stored somewhere within the terrier's cranium? Perhaps not, yet somehow it was made available to Missie and she was sufficiently in tune with this source that she could act as a near-perfect channel.

But to one salesman, at least, Missie was a virtual library. He came knocking on Miss Probert's door, wanting to sell her a set of encyclopedia. "I have a walking one right here," she replied. "What do you want to know?" Once he adjusted himself to the situation and decided to humor his potential buyer, the salesman settled on the subject of the Civil War. He asked a number of questions. Unhesitantly the answers came back from the pint-sized genius before him. "I guess you're right, lady," he said, packing up his samples and shaking his head.

"Dogs can't reason, the scientists say, but Missie did." We could hardly argue with our hostess at this point, sitting mesmerized and just a little numb on our portion of the sofa. Sissie, the dog, jumped up on my lap and wanted to play. I looked into her eyes and for an instant imagined myself peering through these windows into unknown worlds beyond. "She isn't psychic," her owner had said. But I couldn't help wondering. I tossed the ball she held in her mouth. She leaped from my lap in pursuit and I experienced some comfort in that.

"Do you know that Missie always knew what time it was," the voice next to me was saying. "I would say to her, 'Missie, what time is it?' Without bothering to look at the clock, Missie would bark out the hour closest at hand. If I asked her if it was before or after the hour, she would let me know and then bark out the minutes involved.''

"How did you train her to do this?"

"Oh, I didn't train her," Mildred said with an emphatic gesture of her hands. "She did it entirely on her own, just like all the other things. A friend made a play clock for her with hands that could be turned on the face. Sometimes she would prance over to her clock and set the hands where they belonged for the hour. A child might move the hands in any direction, but Missie always moved the hands in a clockwise fashion.''

Mildred leaned back against the overstuffed sofa and sighed. "But Missie was no saint. She wasn't perfect. In so many ways she was like a small child. It was strange that she could be so knowing, so wise, and yet be so childish . . . I say childish, for Missie behaved more like a spoiled child prodigy than a dog.

"She was a ham, always wanting center stage. She loved to show off for people. For that matter, she loved people, all kinds of people, including the truckers that would stop in the alley behind the house. She would stand at the window and throw them kisses by pursing her mouth and then sending it off with a paw. She really made an effort to kiss, not lick like other dogs.

"She could raise a fuss when she wanted something and didn't get it. I would carry her in a little sack when I went shopping and she would be quiet as a churchmouse until she spotted something she wanted, like a small stuffed toy, and particularly if it was pink. Everything had to be pink. Dogs are supposed to be colorblind but Missie wanted everything pink whether it was her toys, flowers, clothes, or her ice cream. But if she wanted something in a store and I didn't get it for her, she would go 'ooo-oo-oo' and kick at me. Twice she shoplifted, dropping something in my sack when I wasn't looking. Then she would deny that she had put it there.

"When visitors came, she would run and get her piggybank, place it in front of them, and then pound on the top of it for dimes. It had to be dimes because she knew that it took a dime to buy a pink ice cream cone from the ice cream man. If you tried to drop something else in, she would grab her bank and run away. When she got her ice cream, she wanted to hold the cone between her paws to eat it. If you put it in her dog pan, she wouldn't have anything to do with it. Even when she was a puppy, she wanted to hold her bottle with her paws. She always had a box of pink chocolates, and when she performed for someone they were expected to give her a chocolate and she wouldn't accept it from anyone else. On one occasion the veterinarian gave her a shot in her fanny, and like people talking about their operations, Missie had to call everyone's attention to her wound by wiggling her fanny at them.''

Mildred thumbed through a scrapbook on her famous dog, and as her eye focused on some item that recalled a particularly fond memory we were forgotten for a moment. Then she glanced at us and smiled wistfully. ''Missie was very conscious of schedules and routines. Everything had to be in its place. Before she went to bed at night—dressed in the pink pajamas that were to be put on her by my mother—the furniture had to be where it belonged. If someone had moved a coffee table, she would put her paws against it and giving her 'ooo-oo' sound try to shove it back in place.

''When she awakened in the mornings and before she got out of bed, she would kind of bow on her forepaws and produce a sound like 'aum-aum-aum,' as though she was chanting. Later we heard the 'aum' chant done by Hindus and it sounded almost identical to Missie's morning song. Every morning she had to have her beads put on. She would then go to the bathroom for her morning chore and then insist that we immediately dispose of the paper. This out of the way, she wanted her jacket put on and it was time for breakfast—buttered pancakes or toast. No butter, take it away! She would eat cereal but she had to be spoonfed. No dog dishes, please.

''When she went to bed, it was imperative that a certain

small stuffed dog be there. Not just any toy would do, and that was her bed dog and it was to remain in the bed. She was very careful with all of her toys and when a visiting dog chewed on one of her stuffed dogs she took it to bed and nursed it. After she played with a toy, she put it up again.

"Each new day was an adventure to Missie and always exciting to me, for I never knew what she would do next. She loved to ride escalators and trains at the amusement park. But one ride was never enough. After the first ride she would raise a fuss, saying 'huh-uh, huh-uh,' until you took her a second time, and then she was ready to get off. One day she saw a boy playing with a hoop and she ran home and got out her ring and tried to play with it as he had. There was always something, like the time she saw a mounted deer head in a store. She had me hold her up so she could kiss it and then kept trying to find the rest of the deer. Somebody gave her a hula skirt. I asked her, 'Do you know what a hula dance is?' She immediately responded, 'uh-huh, uh-huh, woof, woof, woof,' for yes. She started dancing on her two hind legs—she often stood up this way—stomping her feet, and she whirled around so fast that the hula skirt waved in the wind and is blurred in this snapshot, as you can see. As far as I know she had never seen a hula dance unless on television."

As Missie's fame grew her activities and achievements were witnessed by many people. Wisely, Miss Probert obtained many notarized affidavits and received many signed letters. One of these was written by Dennis Gallagher, a member of the Colorado house of representatives and now a state senator. He stated:

"To Whom It May Concern:

"One day in the Spring of 1966, while visiting Miss Mildred Probert, her little Boston Terrier, named My Wee Missie, gave quite a performance for me.

"To my amazement the little dog, when asked by Miss Probert, barked out correctly my social security number, my phone number and address and the number of letters in the street on which I live. She then gave the complete birth date; month and year.

"She responded without hesitation and Miss Probert gave her no clues of any sort. Miss Probert would not have kown these numbered items mentioned above. I can only respond to all this in much the same way someone in Shakespeare's play, Hamlet, Act I, Scene V, says to Horatio, 'There are more things in heaven and earth, Horatio, than are dreamt of in your philosophy.' . . . Respectfully submitted . . ."

Among Missie's many predictions were the wide use of new medical drugs, the use of artificial hearts, and major breakthroughs in the causes and cure of cancer to occur in the 1970s. She predicted the cost to the dollar of the construction of a large educational building. She could tell what grades a student would receive on his report card and the channels that various television shows appeared on.

Only once did Missie predict a person's death, for Mildred discouraged this type of question. The single occasion is best told in the following letter:

"In February 1965 we visited our neighbor Mildred Probert. She had her little clairvoyant Boston Terrier, My Wee Missie, answer some questions for us. She barked out the birth dates of our three daughters very plainly and easily understood. Missie also gave the number of letters in our names and the time of day and her own address, including the zip code number.

"Then my husband put the dog in a chair, leaned over her and asked, 'How many months will I live?' Miss Probert protested. She did not want her dog to predict death, and cautioned littie Missie not to answer that question.

"My husband insisted on the dog answering and would not release her. (He said he felt he would live only a few months—not years.) Missie answered his question with '25.' Miss Probert quickly said 'perhaps she means twenty-five years.'

"He then asked the dog, 'How many years will I live?' Missie answered immediately '2.' He continued, 'Could you tell me the date, the month?' Missie answered '4.' He asked, 'The day?' She replied '3' '1967.'

"This event came true, exactly as the dog predicted. My husband, C. Kincaid, died on April 3, 1967. The fourth month, third day, twenty-five months (two years) later. All the members of our family saw Missie perform her gift of prophesying innumerable times." The letter is signed "Norma Kincaid Price."

Mr. Kincaid had told Mildred that his doctor had told him that he had terminal stomach cancer and would live no longer than three to five months. He had died of accidental gunshot wounds.

Death was predicted by Missie only one other time—her own.

One day in May 1966, a few days before her eleventh birthday, Missie kept calling Mildred's attention to the time, but she would bark eight o'clock. Since it was not that time, Mildred would ask her what time it said on the clock. Missie would then bark the correct time but would immediately go back to barking eight o'clock. She did this seven times that day Mildred recalls. At exactly eight p.m. Missie died, choking on a piece of food. All efforts to save her were to no avail. Later Mildred discovered Missie's toy clock in a corner of the room. The hands had been turned to eight o'clock.

Three weeks later Missie, Mildred, and Missie's veterinarian would have been on their way to Hollywood, where Missie was to star in a Walt Disney film. All arrangements had been made, starting with a publicity banquet in a large Los Angeles hotel in Missie's honor. All decorations were to be done in pink.

"She never looked any older. To the day she died she appeared to be a puppy. Rigor mortis did not set in for thirty-six hours until just before the autopsy. Our veterinarian had called the Colorado School of Veterinary Medicine at Fort Collins to ask if they wanted Missie's brain because of unusual brilliance. They stated they would be quite pleased to receive her brain."

Missie was buried in the back yard of the home. The

pink petunias that she loved were planted on her grave, and though petunias are annuals that die with the first hard frost, these petunias continued to bloom throughout the winter, and the temperature dropped to seventeen degrees below zero. The grave—as shown by several of Mildred's snapshots—has continued to remain green all year.

Silence crept in on us, but there in the old Victorian halls were the echoes of another day. "Ah, Mildred," Jeann'e said, "You must finish the book . . . it has something to say to us all."

I could only nod.

4

Animals in the ESP Laboratories

Sgt. Bill Johnson was returning from Vietnam. He expected to arrive at his home in Newark, New Jersey, on Thursday and he wanted to surprise his family. But his dog, Nellie, spoiled his plans, for somehow she received the message on Wednesday and in unbridled joy rushed around the house collecting personal items belonging to the soldier. These she hauled into the living room, and then she planted herself at the front door and refused to budge until Johnson appeared.

This is a true and not at all unusual story. In the process of researching this book I collected dozens of such stories. As a matter of fact, I soon discovered that all that was really necessary to elicit a story was to mention to anyone who happened to be at hand—the mailman, barber, neighbor, waitress—that I was writing a book on the psychic nature of animals and I stood a fair chance of receiving a response that would start out something like this: "Let me tell you about an incident that happened a couple of years ago with my cat, Socrates . . ."

On a recent trip to Denver I had to get some work done on my car. The mechanic noticed lying on the front seat several books on psychic phenomena and queried if I believed "in that kind of stuff." He quickly added that he certainly didn't put much stock in it himself. But my attempt to discuss some of the serious research in the field was soon interrupted by the man telling one incident after another about his big Labrador reading his mind and about a horse that always knew when to hide when some member of the family was thinking about riding.

There is a mountain of evidence supporting belief in the psychic power of animals—pets aware that their masters have died or are in danger although hundreds of miles away at the time; mindreading feats; predictions of earthquakes, storms, and even bombings hours before they happen; the ability to traverse a continent in the search of a lost master; the returning from the dead to warn former owners of danger; even clairvoyance, as in the strange case of Missie, the Boston terrier whose story is told in the previous chapter. Strange tales of powers that few of us, the "superior" species on this planet, can demonstrate.

Several years ago our next-door neighbor boarded a large Persian cat for her mother, who was visiting friends in England for the summer. The cat and the elderly woman had lived together in an apartment for four years and had not been separated for more than a day or two during that time. So it was understandable that the cat was upset for several days upon being left behind, but she soon adjusted to the new arrangement and seemed reasonably content. But a month after her mistress had left on the trip the cat sat in a corner of the living room meowing piteously, refusing to eat, and ignoring all attention. Shortly after noon of the second day the cat broke into a loud yowling. Within the hour our neighbor received a telephone call that her mother had died enroute to the hospital from a heart attack.

This is no more difficult to explain than how a seven-year-old beagle badly injured by an automobile found its way to the threshold of a veterinarian more than two miles distant, a place he had never been before. What model of intellect can we use to unravel how a horse could spell out correct answers to questions by nudging alphabet blocks with his nose? How can we explain how a St.Bernard could locate a wrecked airplane deep in snow on a mountain slope miles from civilization, or how a mother rabbit hooked to an electroencephalograph could know the very moment that each of her babies was killed aboard a submarine hundreds of miles offshore? The stories are easy to come by; the explanations are scarce.

One thing, at least, is rather evident: Like humans, some animals are apparently psychic and others are not. Some dogs are aware that their master is returning home, others are not; some pets can read their owners' minds, others show little indication of this talent; some animals warn their owners of impending danger, while others just let it happen. People unacquainted with animals have the tendency to group the members of a species or breed under instinct, intelligence, and behavioral categories. They are likely to contend that a cat is a cat and can be expected to exhibit certain qualities. Yet pet lovers will argue vigorously that every animal is as individualistic as humans. While some might point out that a species will demonstrate certain instinctual traits, others will likely use the same argument for human behavior. For that matter, what is instinct? The mere labeling of something hardly explains it, but this question will be reserved for later discussion.

As our concern here is the psychic skills of animals, it might be useful for us to direct our attention to the efforts of several scientific investigators to explore these phenomena. Scientists also have pets, and this sharing, along with the flood of reports of animals not always behaving in the manner that we think they should, occasionally prompted some of these explorers of consciousness to glance at four-footed as well as two-footed creatures. The results have been enlightening. If all cats, or, let's say, all white fluffy cats, were psychic, the task might have been easier for the examiners. But there are cats that predict tomorrow's weather through their behavior, and there are other felines that don't know enough to get in out of the rain. And where these individual qualities of intelligence and virtue lead us is away from any simple classification of brain structure, nervous system, and model of intellect. Such handy comparisons will not serve our turn here. The fact that a German shepherd can display psychic talents beyond those of his peers in the neighborhood or, for that matter, those of his owners has struck some scientists as indeed peculiar. They decided to submit animals to psychic testing in the laboratory.

For laboratory tests, animals are usually placed in simple environments so that the environmental factors influencing the animal can be kept to a minimum. However, this approach fails to provide the investigator with a look at the natural behavior of the animal and undoubtedly this has an effect on the results. Nevertheless the results have been impressive.

Many of the studies provide the subject animal with a set of choices, one of which leads to an outcome desired by the animal. ESP is exhibited, it is believed, if the animal makes a sufficient number of right choices.

At Duke's Parapsychology Laboratory, Karlis Osis and Esther Foster ran a study on kittens placed in a T-shaped maze. The kittens were trained to understand that either arm of the maze could lead to concealed food. The food was then shifted around and the kittens had to decide which arm of the maze contained the food. Olfactory clues were minimized by blowing air away from the cats.

The kittens did well above chance when they were shown affection and when distractions were avoided. Fixed patterns, however, such as having the food on the right or left several times in a row, tended to discourage the animals' effectiveness.

Some studies have used a precognition procedure, in which the choice that will lead to the reward has not yet been made at the time that the animal chooses. C. E. M. Bestall and James Craig have found evidence that rats and mice placed in two-choice mazes are able to predict which of the two choices would later be designated randomly as the correct choice.

The most consistent and important set of animal studies, according to Robert L. Morris, Ph.D., research coordinator of the Psychical Research Foundation in Durham, North Carolina, are those initiated by Pierre Duval and Evelyn Montredon in France and continued in America by Walter Levy with gerbils and hamsters. The animal is placed in a small cage divided into halves by a partition which the animal can easily jump over. Once every minute or so a mild shock is administered for approximately five seconds. A random-number generator electronically selects which side is shocked through the floor. The animal presumably is motivated to anticipate which side is about to be shocked so that it can jump to the nonshocked side. The animal's position is monitored electronically and the data is processed automatically. According to Dr. Morris, more than twenty successful series have been run using variations on the above procedures. There have been only a few failures.

Studies have been carried out to see if animals have psychokinetic abilities—that is, if they can manipulate matter mentally. Helmut Schmidt designed a procedure in which an important part of the animal's environment, such as heat from a lamp or shock through a grid, is regulated by a random-number generator which at specific intervals turns the stimulation on and off. The hypothesis used was that an animal with psychokinetic, or PK, ability will influence the generator to keep the environment pleasant. Schmidt discovered that a lamp heating a cat in a cool environment stayed on more often than would be expected by chance.

In a similar study, Walter Levy found that lamps heating chicks and live chicken eggs in a cool environment also stayed on more often than would be expected by chance. This did not occur when the environment was heated sufficiently, nor did it happen when cooked instead of live eggs were used.

An interesting demonstration of canine ESP was conducted recently at Rockland State Hospital in Orangeburg, New Jersey. The experimenters built two copperlined rooms that were vibration-proof and soundproof. In one of the tests, the owner of two hunting beagles was given an airgun and placed in a room where a slide projector showed pictures of animals he had actually hunted. He was to shoot the gun at the animals. Locked in the other room were the beagles, and they were viewed through a hidden observation panel.

When the hunter fired at a slide of a fierce wildcat, the beagles went wild with excitement even though they were in a separate soundproof and vibration-proof room apart from their owner. Their excitement continued as he fired at other animals on the slides, according to project director Dr. Aristide Esser.

In another experiment, a boxer was attached to an electrocardiograph in one room with his woman owner in a separate room. Without giving the woman any prior warning, a stranger burst into the room, shouting abuse at her and threatening physical violence. She was reportedly genuinely frightened, as can be imagined. Her dog in the other soundproof room must have sensed his owner was in danger for at that very moment his heartbeat became violent.

An experiment with a mother dog and one of her puppies revealed that ESP functions between animals. Both of the dogs had been trained to cower when a rolled piece of paper was raised. The dogs were placed in separate rooms and the younger dog was threatened by a rolled newspaper. He cowered and at the same moment the mother also cowered.

In a newspaper interview, Dr. Esser stated that the tests were convincing evidence that some dogs have telepathic powers. "There is no doubt in my mind that some dogs, particularly those with a close relationship with their owners, have highly developed ESP," he stated. "The power is so strong that I'm sure it could hold the key to understanding human ESP."

Psychic investigators Graham K. and Anita M. Watkins used human-animal interaction in their experiments conducted in 1971. Twelve persons were chosen who had done well on ESP and PK tests. Their assignment was to arouse mice out of anesthesia faster than a control group.

Pairs of mice from the same litter, of the same sex, and of the same size were simultaneously made unconscious in identical etherizers. When unconscious, they were placed in plastic pans and taken to an area in which one of the people was seated. The subject then attempted, at a distance of several feet, to arouse his or her mouse.

The experiments were performed with three different approaches: (1) the subject and mouse were in one room and the control mouse was in a separate room; (2) the subject and both mice were in the same room; and (3) the mice were in the same room and the subject viewed them through a one-way glass from a separate room.

According to Dennis V. Waite, writing in the May 1975 issue of *Probe the Unknown*, the experimental mice required only 87 percent as much time to awaken as the control mice.

Researcher Adrian Parker used positive motivation in experiments with gerbils. Following periods of mild food deprivation, the animals were given opportunities to press one of two keys, one of which provided food. The keys were randomly changed by a computer. The animal was "free to respond at its own pace, making choices whenever it felt so inclined. It may be that animals have flashes of precognition only intermittently, and this schedule allowed them to take full advantage of these," Parker stated.

One of the advantages of the procedures used, according to the researcher, was that when the gerbil did respond, the only information regarding the possible correctness of his response was at the next position on the paper tape which had not yet come into the tape reader and had no effect on the electronic logic. Waite also pointed out that people in the room with the animal could provide no clues because they had no way of knowing which key was the right one. They couldn't see the parts of the tape about to enter the machine's reader. The randomness of the tapes was rechecked after runs.

"There was a significant problem: an overestimate of actual trials since within-trials (before the keys were reactivated) were also counted even though they never led to reward. There was also 'some ambiguity' in the number of responses since the gerbils tended to 'attack' the keys after they had missed the food for several times in a row.

"Nevertheless," Waite continued, "the animals obtained significantly more than chance number of rewards (55 percent). Different animals also scored in various levels of success."

In some ways the mystery of animal behavior is considerably less than it was several years ago. A leading animal behavior researcher, Nikko Tinbergen, has stated: "If one applies the term (ESP) to perception by process not yet known to us, then extrasensory perception among living creatures may well occur widely. In fact, the echolocation of bats, the function of the lateral line in fishes and the way electric fishes find their prey are all based on processes which we did not know about—and which were thus 'extrasensory' in this sense—only 25 years ago."

Yet, there are many kinds of animal behavior which clearly meet the definition of extrasensory perception— that is, the animal will be aware of events, conditions, etc., that cannot be traced to our present knowledge of the five senses. At this point there is little reason to believe that extrasensory perception in animals is different than it is in humans. It would seem safe to assume that when we learn more about extrasensory perception and psi (a Greek letter used generically for all types of psychic phenomena) our knowledge can be applied to both animal and human subjects. If, for example, we discover that awareness of consciousness is not something that is a product of the mechanical-chemical function of the body and not something limited by the space-time structure of the body, then the explanation of ESP may not reside in the body-organic brain-nervous system, but on other levels. In this case the differences—if they exist—between animal and human paranormal abilities cannot be found merely by studying the differences in physical systems.

One area of study of extrasensory perception in animals has to do with psi trailing cases. Homing is a familiar phenomenon. A creature such as a homing pigeon is taken from its home in a closed container and then released many miles distant, and it will find its way back to its home. It is believed that homing involves cues from star and sun positions, geomagnetic field gradients, and so on, which enable the animal to determine where it is in relation to its target. This phenomenon, however, does not explain how animals can find their way to an unknown target or to places they have never been.

In psi trailing, the animal finds its way to a new place never visited before and of which it knows nothing. One of the most famous stories regarding this talent is about a young female collie, Bobbie. She was driving with her family from Ohio to their new home in Oregon, a place where Bobbie had never been. During a stop in Indiana, Bobbie wandered away and after an exhaustive search by the family they finally had to give up and continue on their journey.

Nearly three months later, a skinny and somewhat battered Bobbie showed up on the doorstep of the new Oregon home. In addition to the collar, there were several identifying marks and scars. A man by the name of Charles Alexander read about Bobbie's journey in a newspaper and he determined to follow her trail from Indiana to Oregon. Alexander placed ads in strategically located newspapers and found a number of people who claimed to have temporarily cared for a collie of Bobbie's description. When the trail was mapped out it was found that Bobbie picked a very reasonable route with few detours.

J. B. Rhine and Sara Feather have surveyed fifty-four psi-trailing cases from their files in the Parapsychology Laboratory. The cases were chosen because they met their criteria of providing a reliable source of information; a specific characteristic, such as a nametag or identifiable scar; general sense and internal consistency of the case; and adequate supporting data, such as independent corroboration of testimony, availability of the animal for inspection, etc. Four of the cases involved birds and the remainder were with dogs and cats. Twenty-five of the cases involved distances of more than thirty miles. While fifty-four cases may not be a large number, they lend considerable support to the presence at least in some animals of psi-trailing ability.

Another area of investigation of unusual perception in animals has to do with apparitional cases and with haunted places. The stories are many of dogs howling upon the death of some person. The abilities of animals to be aware of ghosts, disincarnate beings, etc., will be related in a later chapter, but we might mention here that psychic investigators have been known to take dogs, cats, or other animals along as they are believed to be more sensitive to subtle fields than humans. Raymond Bayless and Ernesto Bozzano have written several books dealing with this matter, and Dr. Robert Morris, mentioned earlier, in an informal study reported that a friend took a dog, cat, rat, and rattlesnake to an allegedly haunted house having two "bad vibes" rooms in which murders had been committed. "When introduced to one of these rooms, the dog, cat, and snake reacted as though they were being threatened. The rat remained quite calm. None of the four animals reacted out of the ordinary when introduced to one of the other rooms in the house which had no comparable past history. Of additional interest is that when humans entered the 'bad vibes' room, they reported a temperature drop, estimated by one to be about 20 degrees Fahrenheit; an actual thermometer recorded no temperature drop at all," Dr. Morris relates in an article, "Animals and ESP," written for the October 1973 issue of *Psychic*.

The Psychical Research Foundation has initiated studies using animals as responders in out-of-body experience (OOBE) studies. Gerbils, dogs, hamsters, and cats have been used in these experiments. In preliminary studies it was found that a cat owned by a person who was being tested for OOBE became intensely quiet during the time it was being "visited" by its owner. It was found that the cat's quiet time coincided with that pinpointed by the OOBE'er as being the period he had visited his pet. More on these experiences later.

Some research has centered around the testing of animals that have displayed unusual degrees of higher intelligence. Occasionally in one country or another an animal will emerge that apparently can do rather complex arithmetic, spell out intelligent sentences, and do various kinds of ESP tricks. Most of these are dogs and horses which have been taught to respond to gestures or verbal questioning. They usually perform by selecting by nose or mouth lettered or numbered blocks or by tapping out the answers or, in the case of dogs, by barking.

Perhaps the best-known horse to perform in this manner was Clever Hans. The German horse baffled audiences and scientists alike until it was discovered that Hans couldn't perform unless someone was present who knew the correct answer. Hans was such a careful observer of those around him that he apparently was cued by the head positions of observers. When he started tapping his answers, those present would lean forward to get a good view. Once the horse had tapped the correct number of times, those who knew the answer would involuntarily relax and lean back again and thus indicate to Hans when to stop. If these cues were not available to Hans, he would keep on tapping until tired or until cued by some other signal.

But a number of other animal performers have not been so easy to figure out. Supposedly, Durov, a Russian animal trainer, for a number of years was able to demonstrate telepathy between himself and his animals to the satisfaction of scientists who investigated the phenomena. We will take a closer look at some of these highly unusual animals and their feats later, some of which demand a reassessment of our theories concerning animal intelligence. Missie, the clairvoyant terrier, presents us with a myriad of baffling questions, as does the intelligent interchange between Fred Kimball and Beatrice Lydecker and a host of four-legged conversants.

The Elberfield horses are not easy to explain, and Lady, a horse owned by Mrs. Claudia Fonda, performed some remarkable ESP feats. The Rhines twice investigated the horse, and initially found the animal capable of what appeared to be true ESP performance. Later, however, the scientists found the horse only able to produce when given access to cues. One of the most thoroughly researched animals was Chris the Wonder Dog. He was owned by George Wood and was investigated during the late 1950s by Remi Cadoret at the Parapsychology Laboratory at Duke. Chris would respond to verbal questions by pawing the correct answers on Wood's forearm. Wood taught Chris to guess which of five standard ESP symbols were enclosed in opaque envelopes. He pawed once for circle, two for cross, and so on. Chris reportedly was able to run through a pack of twenty-five cards with a very high degree of accuracy even though no one else knew the order of the cards, thereby seemingly ruling out the possibility that the dog was receiving the messages telepathically.

Yet, when Cadoret endeavored to repeat the performance, an interesting thing happened—Chris' score dipped way below chance. This often happens with human ESP subjects and is thought to be due to negative psychological factors. Some investigators have used this phenomenon to argue that animal ESP is similar or identical to human ESP, while others contend that animals such as Chris are being telepathically cued by their owners who may not be aware of their own ESP abilities. In any case these animals would have to be responsive to telepathic messages.

J. B. Rhine suggests three other categories of human-animal psi communications: a reaction to the distant distress or death of the animal's owner; anticipation of a positive event such as the return home of the owner after a long absence; and a reaction to impending danger either to the animal itself or to the animal's owner.

As an example of the above, Dr. Morris cites the case of a dog being quartered by a veterinarian while the owners were some distance away vacationing in Florida. The dog started howling uncontrollably one morning at ten a.m. and continued for an hour. Examination revealed nothing wrong with the dog. When the owners were told of the incident, they explained that during that precise time they were stranded on top of their car during a flash flood. They were rescued at eleven a.m.

Investigators continue to ponder whether humans can infuence the behavior of lower animals, in a sense "willing" them to bark so many times, turn in one direction rather than another, etc. Studies have been carried out with everything from bats to butterfly larvae and sufficient evidence has been produced to indicate that something is going on. But some have made a case for psychokinesis in humans, while others have contended that the results clearly reveal ESP in animals. More than likely, definitive answers will not emerge until we know more about psi in general. At the moment it seems to be reasonable to assume that animal owners can have psychokinetic powers and that animals do have ESP abilities. For that matter, how do we know that animals are not willing us to turn in a desired direction or telepathically informing us that it is time to eat?

In concluding his article, Dr. Morris stated: "The evidence from anecdote and experiment that ESP is present in other species besides our own is considerable. Results with animals are at least as positive and consistent as human results, probably much more so. The only conclusive refutation of elaborate counter-explanations involving experimenter psi, etc., is the development of a large body of interrelated facts about the exact processes involved. I think the beginnings of such may be at hand . . ."

Discussing the implications of psi research with animals, Dr. Morris explained, "The finding of considerable evidence for psi in animals already has one important implication. It tells us that psi is apparently not of recent evolution . . ."

There are some other implications that can be drawn. The evidence on hand would seem to indicate that there is an awareness beyond the so-called normal senses. This awareness puts the subject not only in contact with his immediate environment but also with things and events at some distance. This awareness may be shared by not only humans and animals but all living things. If this should happen to be the case, then life, regardless of the form it takes, would seem to be enveloped by a universal and unifying consciousness. Each thing would be related to everything else, and each life form would to some minute degree be affecting and influencing everything in the universe. These possibilities and some ways of looking at psychic abilities will be explored in the following chapter.

5

Animals and Pyramid Phenomena

Beyond the edge of history, man built the pyramids on the Giza plain of Egypt. How far back no one really knows. They are the only surviving monoliths of a once great civilization long since reduced to dust by the changing sands of the Sahara or perhaps swallowed by the waters of the Atlantic.

Did these mountains grow there by the Nile nourished for days and years by slaves forced to raise a tomb unto some vainglorious king, or were they the inspired creation of mental giants fired with the light of erecting on earth the very knowledge of the universe? Who? Why? How? When?

The questions can be raised, but the answers are limited to conjecture. Whatever the answers they are not likely to be the right ones. Peering back at man's attempts over the centuries to explain the riddles of his world, one realizes that every answer offered about the nature of something — what it is, how it works—sooner or later is set aside by a new conclusion. This is the way it has been and this is the way it is likely to be for some time to come. The human mind simply has not evolved to the point where it can totally comprehend anything. It is our lot to be content with trading fragments for bigger and better fragments.

But the game goes on and with it the dream of discovering more tomorrow.

Beside the pyramids stands the Sphinx, silent sentinel of the passing parades, the touch of an enigmatic smile playing along the corners of lips frozen less by stone than by silence. Part beast, part man, part god, symbolic perhaps of the soul on a journey . . . an animal on the way to becoming a god? We ponder and find more joy in our poetry than our experiments, for man is also a mystic. Or perhaps he was a mystic before he was a man; soaring high in the heavens on eagle's wings or listening to the whispers of nature beside a mountain den, how close then to the reality of things?

We are not always sure of the origin of our discoveries, whether they come to us from our long-forgotten past, or are the product of the rational mind, or are inspirations from having for a moment touched the divine. Questions asked sooner or later bear fruit. The fruit may not last, but while it does it serves as nourishment for another step. Antoine Bovis had paused beside the Sphinx before passing on to the Great Pyramid. He was still wondering about the strange combination of man and beast depicted in the huge statue when he entered the King's Chamber. Maybe it was this thought that made him notice a small dead animal in one corner of the room. He was fascinated by the discovery that the creature—obviously long dead—had not deteriorated but had simply mummified.

Something told Bovis that one of the secrets of this occurrence was the shape of the pyramid, that the shape altered the energy fields inside in such a manner that instead of rotting the animal dehydrated. He tested this hypothesis when he returned home to France. He built model pyramids, constructed to the scale of the Great Pyramid and also aligned on the north-south axis. Dead animals placed inside the models at a location approximating that of the King's Chamber mummified without spoiling. The French experimenter had launched the new era of pyramid construction.

His studies came to the attention of a Czechoslovakian

radio engineer named Karl Drbal. Interested in wave fields, crystals, and so on, Drbal wondered what influence pyramid space would have on metal structures, and he found that razor blades could be resharpened if placed inside model pyramids. His patented pyramid razor-blade sharpeners came to the attention of two American reporters on tour of the iron-curtain countries in pursuit of new scientific discoveries. They mentioned the pyramid experiments in their book, *Pychic Discoveries Behind the Iron Curtain*, and started a craze for pyramidology in this and a number of other countries. Interest grew as investigators—from basement tinkerers to professional researchers—found that unusual phenomena did, indeed, occur inside pyramids.

It might be reaching too far to suggest that the small creature sacrificed itself inside the Great Pyramid in order to call man's attention to new dimensions of energy fields. But animals have wittingly or unwittingly given themselves upon man's scientific altars, and without their contributions scientific knowledge would be a far cry from what it is today.

Ed Pettit and I were two of those bitten by the pyramid bug. Our research over a four-year period included experiments with hundreds of plants, liquids, solids, with pyramids of many sizes and materials under a variety of conditions. Our work culminated in two books, *The Secret Power of Pyramids* and *The Psychic Power of Pyramids*, but looking back it can be seen that animals played critical roles in our efforts. They were directly responsible for new directions and for the working hypotheses as they developed.

A small female gerbil set the stage for many experiments that followed. Shortly after proving to ourselves that razor blades could be kept sharp inside of pyramids, and that fruit, vegetables, meat, eggs, milk, etc., could be preserved therein without spoilage, we decided to place the small creature inside a pyramid to see what would happen. No brilliant scheme was involved, just curiosity, but the results now make us wonder if we weren't being directed by designs other than our own.

The gerbil was jubilant. She had never before displayed such abundant joy. She ate better, grew some, although already mature, and soon exhibited a luxurious coat of fur. And such tranquillity; nothing would upset her. Of particular note was her new interest in housekeeping chores. She cleaned up her cage and made her nest neatly in one corner instead of having it strewn over half the cage as before. But when her cage was removed from the pyramid, she became quite upset. She refused to eat and her household was soon a mess. Back under the pyramid and she was happy again.

One day she cut herself badly on her cage. The gash was so deep near one eye we thought she might lose it. The wound was not treated but she was kept under the pyramid. Healing took place rapidly and the gash closed without so much as leaving a scar.

Our experiences with the gerbil encouraged us to build pyramids large enough for people to sit, meditate, and even sleep in. This opened up a whole new field of adventure. Our experiments with smaller pyramids had provided us with some exciting results, but the larger pyramids permitted us to test ourselves and others in a variety of ways. As the results were shared with friends and with others through correspondence, newspapers, and radio and television interviews, many people started building larger pyramids, and they, in turn, shared their experiences with us. In this manner we were able to collect considerable data on persons experiencing pyramid space.

Briefly—for this material was covered in *The Psychic Power of Pyramids*—people reported feeling peaceful and tranquil inside pyramids. They felt removed in a comfortable sort of way from the distractions of the outside world and isolated even though separated only to the extent of a sheet of plastic or plywood. Their meditation was better, easier to get into and maintain, than it was outside. A ''presence'' was felt inside the pyramids, one that subjects found difficult to describe as it was not the feeling that their space was being shared by some disincarnate being or invisible personality but more like a beneficial, caring sort of force. And it was exciting to discover that irritations and problems carried into the pyramid could not be sustained for long inside. Their troubles seemed to fade away, and one subject told us that he even made a serious effort to hold and project feelings of hostility but found it impossible. One sensitive soul told us that she entered the pyramid carrying the burdens of the world, completely depressed by "the mess that the world was in." She left an hour later with feelings of hope and even optimism.

So our happy, jubilant gerbil had grown to a crowd of more contented people. Even those suffering from claustrophobia felt comfortable in the wonder of pyramid space. "Housekeeping chores" also emerged with a new style for many individuals. Greater enthusiasm was discovered in the day-to-day business of living, as projected by our furry little crystal ball. Individuals found themselves singing and whistling again and reducing mountains back into molehills. Many phone calls and letters related how a new inner poise had been found, while more than a few told us they had been able to "get it back together again."

But perhaps the most amazing experiences had to do with healing. On two different occasions Ed Pettit badly damaged his hands with power tools; the second time his right hand was so severely torn the attending physician thought he would lose the last joints of two fingers. He spent a great deal of time in a pyramid in both instances. As a result of the first healing experience, Pettit was convinced the pyramid would pull him through again. The fingers were saved, and, although there is no way to know if the pyramid was the cause, the doctor was so amazed with the rapid improvement that he furnished us a signed statement for our book.

No sooner had this occurred, however, than we started hearing from people all over the country telling us about their healing experiences with pyramids. While we cannot represent pyramid models as devices of healing, we can share the experiences. People have been telling us of cuts, bruises, broken bones, etc., healing in much less time; scar tissue disappearing; arthritis and rheumatism being alleviated; headaches and ulcers fading away; skin problems clearing up . . . the list seems endless.

Pyramids, the miracle workers? We do not know. We have asked ourselves and others many questions having to do with energy fields, belief systems, positive thinking, suggestion (although many of the correspondents were not aware of other people's healing experiences), electromagnetic influences, and so on. There was a time when we pondered if the changes weren't the result of psychosomatic factors, having little to do with organic systems as such. And once again the experience with our gerbil took on a new significance.

We said to one another that the apparent healing couldn't be simply of a psychosomatic nature if the unusual healing of the small creature meant anything. This question was poised in midair when we started noticing that Pettit's dog, Wolf, who had been voluntarily spending some time each day in an outside pyramid for several weeks, was limping less from an arthritic condition and was wanting to play ball again, something he had refrained from doing for more than a year. Then, as if by design, further confirmation arrived in the form of letters and phone calls: "Let me tell you what the pyramid has done for my pet," they said.

It seemed that most of our reporters had constructed large pyramids for their own designs only to discover that their cats, dogs, rabbits, squirrels, parrots, whatever, had other plans for the household or back-yard furnishing. They moved in at every opportunity, attracted by some mysterious force to the pyramid. Whatever message the animals were receiving, they were allegedly feeling better from an assortment of ailments, were more vigorous, coats or feathers more luxurious, and they seemed more contented.

Why the animals were attracted to the pyramids raises some interesting questions. It seems safe to assume that the creatures experienced in some fashion the same sensations as humans—quietude, peace, and invigoration. Animals, more attuned to nature than ourselves, are more responsive to those things which are good for them and avoid things which are harmful. They can be found chewing on grass and herbs when their systems are out of balance and will fast and rest when they are ill. Most primitive medicines were discovered by watching animals eat certain plants for different problems. The plants were tried by man and slowly his stock of remedies has grown over the centuries. Most of the medicines we have today were derived in this fashion, but they were first discovered by other animals.

With their inborn sense of selection, it is not likely that animals will voluntarily choose conditions which are not beneficial to them. Do they know the pyramids have healing powers? We have no way of knowing, of course, but something attracts them. They will choose a pyramid over an established resting place. When a pyramid is closed, they often will lie on the outside next to the structure. A parrot that escaped from his cage was found several hours later sitting on top of a six-foot wooden pyramid five blocks from his home.

Bill Kerrell and Kathy Goggin suggest in *The Guide to Pyramid Energy* giving water treated in pyramids to pets, claiming that if an animal is given a choice, it will choose the treated water. They also note that when their tomcat comes home with battle wounds he will head for the pyramid constructed for their pets and will not come out for twenty-four hours. "Even severe wounds seem to heal with amazing speed during these therapy sessions," they explain.

Kerrell and Goggin have tested the life span of brine shrimp under pyramids as compared to controls and have produced some exciting results. "We have hatched at least a dozen batches of these shrimp, each time with much the same results," they state. "Being sure that both the hatch under the pyramid and the control batch are in environments as close to identical as possible, we have found that pyramid water and a pyramid over the test tank can greatly extend the lives of the shrimp." The controls lived a maximum of seven weeks, but the shrimp under the pyramid were still living after one year.

Tom Garrett, a psychology student in Oklahoma City, has had much the same luck with small exotic fish in an aquarium. Instead of the aquarium being under a pyramid, however, four-inch solid plastic pyramids were placed inside on the bottom of the water tank. The fish thrived, set new records in reproduction, and grew to larger than normal size. Any film residue disappeared from the sides of the tank and from the gravel in the bottom. In fact, the water became so crystal clear, "like liquid ice," Garrett stated, that he disconnected the aquarium's filter system. It has now been several months, but the water has remained fresh and clear. Ed Pettit has repeated Garrett's experiments with much the same results. One experiment with fish and pyramids, however, produced something less than a beneficial result, at least for the fish. Garrett placed a solid plastic pyramid underneath an aquarium with the top of the apex touching the bottom of the tank. The fish started dying. He removed the pyramid and no additional deaths occurred. The pyramid was reinstalled and several more fish expired before the pyramid was removed. This experiment has not been repeated or confirmed by any other researcher at this writing, but we are planning to do so. At this point we can only speculate that the energy field generated was either too strong for the fish or somehow produced a negative result—something that seldom happens with pyramids.

Pyramid space is apparently a negative field as far as insects are concerned. If they enter a pyramid, they will not remain, according to several reports we have received. Fruit, vegetables, and other food products are not bothered by roaches, flies, and so on within the structures. A friend conducted a test with some ants. Noticing an anthill near his outside pyramid, he placed some breadcrumbs in the middle of the pyramid and an equal amount on the ground outside. The ants soon found their way to the new goodies outside, but the encampment that headed for the pyramid turned back shortly after entering. One brave scout made it to the food and even picked up a crumb, but did not get far before he had to unload and head for a more pleasant environment. Why animals seemingly are attracted to the pyramids and not insects we do not know. We wonder if insects beneficial to man, such as bees, would be affected adversely by pyramid space. It shouldn't be too difficult to explore this question but to date we have not experimented.

Animals with their more acute senses and possibly greater psychic attunement may well be aware of energy fields that man—for the most part—only detects indirectly. Many humans have experienced unusual sensations inside pyramids, but animals may pick up these subtle fields immediately. They may be more responsive because they do not question, rationalize, and analyze as we have a tendency to do.

In any case, it was the dogs and cats that led us to another discovery concerning pyramid space. We noticed that whenever our dogs entered the pyramid they always lay down in the northeast corner. We failed to give this much attention at first since once a dog establishes a place and leaves his scent there, he will generally return to the same spot. But then we started receiving letters and phone calls from people who had made the same observation. A friend decided to test his dog. He rotated his pyramid so that what was the northeast corner became the southwest corner. The dog entered the pyramid, went to the southwest corner and sniffed for a moment, and then went to the northeast corner and lay down.

We wondered what was so attractive about the northeast corner. We decided to try some tests on human subjects. We asked them to enter the pyramid with us and we blindfolded them. We then turned them around a couple of times and told them to continue to turn slowly in a circle until they felt they were facing the direction "that was the most comfortable." When they stopped turning, four out of five were facing an east to northeast direction. A clairvoyant individual sees a particularly bright radiation in the northeast section of the pyramid, and mystics for ages have suggested that people sleep with their heads either to the north or to the east, but never to the south or west. Regardless of the weather or the season the American plains Indian always pitched his teepee with the opening facing east.

The southwest corner of the pyramid does appear to be a place creating negative reactions on the part of both humans and animals. Individuals who have sat in the southwest corner of a pyramid for any length of time report feeling nervous and upset, or have experienced headaches. Without mentioning the unusual quality of the southwest corner, we have invited a small group of people to meditate inside our pyramid. We maneuver the group so that someone ends up sitting in the southwest corner. We have observed that in a very short time this person becomes restless and usually moves to some other location. Later he will say that he moved because he felt "restless," "couldn't seem to settle down," "seemed to be experiencing bad vibrations," and so on. One woman told us she actually felt ill, and another woman left the pyramid during one of the meditation sessions as she felt that "it was closing in on me and I had to get out of there."

Tom Garrett, mentioned earlier, when he first started his experiments, built one large pyramid in which to meditate and conduct his research. He decided to test the dehydration rate of apples and cut one apple in half. He placed one half outside and the other half inside the pyramid one-third of the distance from the base to the apex and directly under the apex. Several days later he found that the apple half outside had turned a dark brown and had some mold on it, but the half inside still appeared fresh. He wanted to meditate inside the pyramid under the apex, and so he temporarily placed the apple in the southwest corner. Less than an hour later, when he had completed his meditation, he picked up the apple to place it back on its pedestal in the middle of the pyramid. "While it may be hard to believe," Garrett explained, "in that short length of time the apple turned completely dark and looked almost as aged as the control apple outside."

There are special places that seem to have an unusual amount of power, and evidently there are other places that seem to radiate negativity. In *The Teachings of Don Juan*, the sorcerer tells Castaneda that each person has a special place and he must find it. If he can locate it, this place will protect him and give him special powers. Alice A. Bailey speaks of special places on earth in her several books. These places, she claims, were part of a grand design of energy fields throughout the earth. They are formed where unusual energy fields cross, forming vortices.

Of the energy grids, John Michell states in *The View Over Atlantis*, "From what we have seen of the scientific methods practised by the adepts of the ancient world it is possible to draw two conclusions. First, they recognized the existence of some force or current, of whose potential we are ignorant, and discovered the form of natural science by which it would be manipulated. Secondly, they gained, apparently by means connected with their use of this current, certain direct insight into fundamental questions of philosophy, the nature of God and of the universe and the relationship between life and death."

Could it be that when a wild animal searches for a special place to build a den or nest, he is monitoring the nature of the energy fields? Humans seem somewhat aware of this when they say that a certain house or place has "good vibrations," or another spot has "bad vibes." Anyone who has had pets will know that occasionally an animal will reject the location chosen for its resting place. It will choose some other spot or else drag its pad or mat to another location even though the original one looked more comfortable to the human eye. I had a dog that rejected his new dog house. I thought he was complaining about the straw I used for his bed, so I changed it. That didn't do it, so again I switched to something else. I noticed, however, that he always lay down in a certain place in his pen. I moved the doghouse to that spot and everything was fine.

This sensitivity is mentioned by Lyall Watson in *Super*

Nature: "The choice of a resting place naturally has to be made very carefully with regard to warmth and shelter and safety from predators, but often an animal will choose a place that seems to be far less appealing on these grounds than another only a short distance away. Domestic dogs and cats show the same behavior, and their owners know full well that it is no good making this decision on the pet's behalf—they have to wait until the animal chooses its own place and then put the sleeping basket there. There are some places on which an animal will not lie on any account.''

Judging from the behavior of a friend's big black Labrador, the pyramid leaves a field behind when it is moved. The friend constructed an eight-foot pyramid at the far end of his property and decided after several months to move it closer to his house. Although the dog had not been allowed inside the pyramid, when the structure was moved to its new location, the Labrador started spending several hours a day lying on the exact spot where the pyramid had stood.

Perhaps some zoo animals are so restless not only because of the obvious factors having to do with their imprisonment but also because they can't find a special place in the small territory allotted to them. One wonders if they would be more contented if they had a pyramid to sleep or spend some time in.

A growing number of people are building or planning to build pyramid houses. They are convinced that the space inside pyramids has special qualities that will enhance their domestic tranquillity. Their faith in this phenomenon has largely been established through observing the health and happiness of animals in such settings. Perhaps our four-footed friends will pioneer a whole new trend in the housing industry.

We have learned a great deal about our world with our questioning mind, our mathematics, test tubes, and microscopes, but the other animals may know of this earth in a way we never learned or else have forgotten. How much greater would be our understanding if we could encompass both ways of knowing? What then would be our realities? Could this have been the reason that the ancient builders saw fit to carve the Sphinx—guardian of the hidden wisdoms of the Giza plain—in the likeness of both man and beast?

6

Animals' Mysterious
Cosmic Clocks

While living in Denver a number of years ago my next-door neighbor shared his small bungalow with a very large black cat, Henry. My neighbor was a widower and not disposed toward conversation, but the cat was gregarious when it came to people. Perhaps Henry became bored with the lack of stimulating interchange in his own household, for he spent his mornings making the social rounds.

Henry would punctually arrive on my doorstep at seven a.m. Why he had chosen this hour I do not know, but maybe he knew that by this time I would have had a cup of coffee and would be sufficiently awake to be civil to a caller. If he waited longer, I would be rushing around getting ready for work, and Henry didn't like to be ignored. If you attempted to do so, he would land in your lap and push his face into yours until you recognized his existence.

Approximately ten minutes after the hour Henry would end our little social interplay and stomp out the door, careful not to miss his next appointment. I learned from the neighbors that he was equally punctual with them, somehow learning or knowing when it was most appropriate to call.

One of the most fascinating aspects of Henry's tight schedule, however, was his attendance at a local auction house. The auction house was less than two blocks away and every Thursday evening at seven p.m. people gathered for the selling of furniture, appliances, tools, etc. Henry never missed this weekly festivity. He knew when it was Thursday, and it was not a matter of being attracted by the crowd, for he would arrive fifteen minutes ahead of the crowd, perch himself atop a wooden file cabinet, and from there watch the entire proceedings.

In the chapter on Missie, the clairvoyant terrier, mention is made of Missie's ability to tell time accurately and to prophesy the exact time of her own death. The case of the Denver dog owned by Mildred Probert is, of course, highly unusual, yet a growing amount of evidence would seem to indicate that all life forms are aware of the cosmic web and its time-clock ticking out the cycles of their destinies.

"All living organisms exist in the pulsating sea of energies serving as receivers, transformers, and projectors," Vincent and Margaret Gaddis state in *The Strange World of Animals and Pets*. "There is a universal electric field affecting all life, while in turn all life exerts its own influence upon the field. Thus each human being, animal and plant is related to all other life, to the earth's magnetic field, and through it to the changes in the electrical fields of the moon and sun . . . All of us who live are a part of the universal whole, fellow creatures in the cosmos, responding to the ceaseless ebb and flow of the universe. And there are other voices from out of the deep that speak in languages still unknown to man."

The idea of a pulsating sea of energy in which everything is enmeshed is not a new one. The ancient Chinese said that man is linked to the cosmos through vital energy which fills the universe. In India they refer to this force as *prana*, in which everything is enveloped. Mesmer called it animal magnetism. Reichenbach referred to it as odic force. Keely named it motor force. Blondot called it N-rays. Soviet scientists have entitled it bioplasmic energy; and Czech scientists call it psychotronic energy. While different names are used, there appears to be general agreement as to the characteristics of this energy. It is being discussed here because it is believed that greater knowledge of newly discovered energy fields and their behavior will provide us some insight into the mysteries of cosmic clocks, of which so many life forms seem to be aware.

Czech scientists Zdenek Rejdak and Karl Drbal have written: "Human beings and all living things are filled with a kind of energy that until recently hasn't been known to Western science. This bioenergy, which we call psychotronic energy, seems to be behind PK; it may be the basis of dowsing. It may prove to be involved in all psychic happenings."

The universal nature of the energy field, indicating that it is shared by all living things, was borne out by the unusual experiments of Cleve Backster, founder of the Backster School of Lie Detection in New York. A recognized expert with the polygraph, Backster demonstrated with a number of carefully planned experiments that plants respond to the thoughts, emotions, and actions of people and animals around them. Death of living things, such as shrimp or fish, occurring in the vicinity of the plants produced an intense reaction on the polygraph. "It seems to indicate some sort of primary perception or consciousness in every living cell," Backster reported.

Since 1930, H. S. Burr and F. S. C. Northrup have carefully examined, in the biological domain, the vital energies of organisms. They considered that there must be some force behind the living organisms in their ability to direct, organize, and hold together the complex chemical interchanges which accompany biological processes. Burr and Northrup have published a number of articles dealing with fields in primitive organisms as well as in trees and animals.

In a monograph entitled *The Energy Field in Man and Nature*. New York psychiatrist John Pierrakos stated: "In nature there are several groups of unicellular organisms; such as bacteria and fungi, and also multicellular structures; such as flagellates, sponges, fish, and fireflies that are able to emit light and 'luminate' as the result of their inner movements and biological processes. In higher organisms, it is known that vital processes such as mitosis of cells, oxidation, and other metabolic processes are accompanied by luminescence. Living organisms are able to emit light through the entire surface of their bodies; they have not lost their ability to luminate. This phenomenon constitutes the energy field, or Aura, which is, in effect, a reflection of the energies of life processes . . . The field phenomena belong, in addition, to another dimension.They are energetic phenomena that transcend the physical realities of matter and, even though they are tied up with the structure and matter of the body, they have their own laws of pulsatory movement and vibration not yet understood.''

It may be that the energy field shared by all living things is, in the final analysis, consciousness, as discussed earlier. This intimate sharing of all that is, whether referred to as energy or consciousness, relates everything to everything. At some level of awareness, either below or beyond cognitive reasoning, life forms are aware of their universe—gravitational forces, magnetic fields, light waves, electromagnetic forces, energy field levels, movements of planetary bodies, solar flares, etc.—all the multiple and largely invisible forces that trigger a knowledge of the hour and the seasons.

A number of years ago there was a patient at the Winfield (Kansas) State Hospital and Training Center for the mentally retarded who was a whiz at telling time. This patient was so severely retarded that he could not cope with even the most elementary demands of his life. Yet, he could be asked at any time during the day or night what time it was and he could say without looking at a watch or clock.

The son of a close friend learned to perform just as well. In his early teens the boy discovered he could tell the time without looking at a timepiece. He was a bright and ingenuous youngster and tried his skills on automobile odometers. Without doing any figuring whatsoever and not knowing in advance the extent to which the family car would be used, he could accurately predict the mileage reading on any projected day. He did not know how he did this but assumed that some cosmic intelligence had all the answers and he was simply somehow tapping this source.

Being in tune with the World Mind might explain how a dog could distinguish Saturdays from the other days of the week. Novelist Frances Parkinson Keyes tells the story of Zip, a pit-bull terrier that belonged to the city treasurer of Baton Rouge, Louisiana. Zip was allowed the run of the city's business district, of City Hall, and he enjoyed riding on the hood of his master's car. Then people started complaining about too many dogs running loose in the city, and so the city fathers passed an ordinance restraining dogs. They hired a dogcatcher to round up the strays.

As luck would have it, Zip was one of the first canines rounded up. He spent the night in the pound and was rescued the following day by his master. To prevent further problems, Zip was placed on a farm several miles out in the country. He had to be chained but the farmer fed him well and tried to make him comfortable. Zip accepted his confinement well until Saturday came. All during the weekend, however, he howled and fought his chain in efforts to gain his freedom. Come Monday he showed every sign of being contented, but the following Saturday the same behavior occurred.

The farmer called the city treasurer and after a conference they decided that the dog knew when Saturday arrived. This was the day in particular that Zip was allowed to ride about with his master. The two men also decided that the dog may have figured out that he could be free on Sundays to roam his old haunts as the dogcatcher wouldn't be working.

The following Saturday, Zip was released, and around

noon he disappeared and was still missing Sunday night. But early Monday morning he was back at the farm barking a greeting. Having demonstrated his responsibility, Zip was given the freedom of the farm. All week long he drove cattle, served as a watchdog and a companion of the farmer. But on Saturdays he took off for town and usually arrived at his master's home around three o'clock in the afternoon. He would stay in town all weekend but was promptly back at the farm shortly after daybreak. According to Mrs. Keyes, this routine continued unbroken for years.

Maurice Burton relates in *The Sixth Sense of Animals* that there is a particular street corner in London where every Tuesday at noon there was a man with his cart loaded with cat meat. He would carve the meat and deliver it to surrounding houses. The unwanted scraps were tossed to the cats that had assembled. Every Tuesday the cats could be seen arriving shortly before noon, anticipating the feast that awaited them. More than a dozen cats would show up and they would sit on the curb together waiting for their benefactor to arrive. The cats never gathered on any other day.

Stories such as this one have convinced pet owners that animals have a sense of time and they have led scientists to search for a biological clock. Man has long observed that there is a rhythm linked to the rotation of the earth: the behavior of plants and animals to the time of the day and the seasons. More than two thousand years ago Androsthenes observed that the foliage of certain plants follows certain daily patterns. And Aristotle found that the ovaries of sea urchins grew in size during times of the full moon.

The most fundamental biological clock produces the approximate twenty-four-hour rhythm. This is known as the circadian rhythm. "Circadian" means "about a day," and the rhythm varies with life forms from twenty-two to twenty-five hours. The circadian rhythm is linked to more than twenty different processes in some animals. Bees, for example, have been found to return to a feeding station at approximately the same time each day. The small Pacific coast fish the grunion follows the waves onto the beach at night from April through June right after the tides reach their monthly peaks. The grunions deposit their eggs in the sand, and this allows the baby fish to develop over a period of a month without being washed out to sea by the surf.

Every living marine animal is aware of the rhythm of the sea. A small flatworm, for instance, is in partnership with green algae and whenever the tide goes out it comes up from the sand and exposes its greenery to the sun. Rachel Carson, author of *The Sea Around Us*, took some of these flatworms into a laboratory and described their conditioning to the tidal rhythm: "Twice each day Convoluta rises out of the sand in the bottom of the aquarium, into the light of the sun. And twice each day it sinks again into the soil. Without a brain, or what we would call a memory, or even very clear perception, Convoluta continues to live out its life in this alien place, remembering, in every fibre of its small green body, the tidal rhythm of the distant sea."

Most ocean animals are observed in laboratories close to the sea. But one researcher of natural rhythms lives a thousand miles from the ocean, in Evanston, Illinois, just outside Chicago. Frank Brown started working with oysters in 1954 and found that they had a marked tidal rhythm, biologist Lyall Watson tells us in *Supernature*. The oysters opened their shells to feed at high tide and closed them to prevent damage and drying out during the ebb of the tide. Even in the Chicago suburb the oysters continued to remember the tidal rhythm of the Connecticut coast.

After two weeks, however, Brown discovered that a small change occurred in the rhythm. The oysters were no longer opening and closing according to the tidal pattern of their home shore. He stated in his report, "Persistent Activity Rhythms in the Oyster," published in *The American Journal of Physiology*, that what was amazing was that all of the oysters had altered their rhythm to the same extent and were keeping time with each other. Finally, Brown figured it out. His calculations revealed that the oysters were opening at the exact time the tide would have flooded Evanston had it been located on the shore instead of being perched on the bank of Lake Michigan nearly six hundred feet above sea level.

Brown wondered if the difference in the time of sunrise and sunset was cueing the oysters, but he found that it made no difference whatsoever if the oysters were kept in dark containers from the time they were taken from the sea.

The fiddler crab has his own individual reaction to tidal rhythm. The crab is darker in color when first exposed at low water and lighter at high tide. These changes continue when it is placed in an aquarium, and is believed to be the result of expansion and contraction of pigment cells in the skin. When pieces of tissue containing the pigment cells are extracted from the crab and kept alive for a time, they will continue to show the same expansion and contraction and change color in timing with the tides. These findings would seem to indicate that even individual cells play a role in the timekeeping process and would tend to support Backster's concept of cellular consciousness.

The sensitivity of marine life to extremely subtle changes in environment may have great significance for all forms of life, including the human one. The lobster may prove to be an effective early-warning system for water pollution. While gross amounts of pollution are visible to anyone, the long-term implications of oil pollution, for example, are largely unknown.

"There may be subtle, low-level effects, and it is at this point that the lowly lobster, creeping along the bottom like an oversized, armored insect, comes into the picture. For it is widely feared that tiny amounts of oil, far below the immediately toxic level, may severely interrupt the complex environment in which such marine organisms feed, migrate and spawn," Michael Schofield stated in an article, "The Smelly Factor," written for the August 1972 issue of *The Smithsonian* and republished by *Intellectual Digest* in February 1973.

Schofield reported on the work of two young oceanographers at Woods Hole Oceanographic Institution on Cape Cod. John Todd and Jelle Atema had been studying animal communication for several years and had learned that minute amounts of foreign substance could vastly alter the behavior of marine life. The scientists introduced kerosene-soaked bricks into a lobster tank. It caused "the lobsters to increase their aggression at times or retreat at others and, in some cases, compulsively clean themselves. When a few drops of either kerosene or oil were introduced into the tank, one lobster did not eat for a week . . ."

In his concluding remarks Schofield laments the lack of knowledge of the effects of pollutants, ". . . effects that are not seen because to us their occurrence is invisible, and thus distant and far removed. But much more immediate is the presence of an undersized lobster, crouching in the back of a water-filled tank, refusing to eat in a small laboratory at Woods Hole. The movement, or lack thereof, of a tiny sensing hair confronted by an infinitely small molecule of oil may have immense implications for humanity."

The manner in which various life forms respond to their environment, whether this is through mechanical, chemical, electrical, or some completely unknown means, is obviously not just a question of an academic nature. If an animal's sensitive tuning devices are distorted, it could alter its behavior and its chances for survival. One remembers recent reports of bears in national parks acting aggressively toward visitors and of sharks attacking humans with a viciousness peculiar in the annals of such events. If a lobster can become unnaturally aggressive as the result of tiny bits of alien material being injected into its environment, one questions if pollutants, and the bombardment by all types of radio waves, might not be affecting the behavior of some animals. Few things would seem to alter an animal's response to its biological clock. However, if this were to happen, what might we expect in changes from the animal kingdom? For that matter, humans, too, are members of that kingdom, and before passing on we might ponder to what extent pollutants—be they chemical, electrical, or whatever—are affecting our health and behavior. Again, if we can believe the new physics, everything in the universe is related and nothing is isolated. As humans, our welfare is not independent of nature. The study of biological clocks provides strong evidence that life's various forms are linked together in the thoughts, the heartbeats, and the breath of the universe.

The attunement to a cosmic clock is illustrated in the case of warblers. In a study conducted during the early 1960s at Freiburg, Germany, E. G. F. Sauer hatched and hand-reared a number of warblers in soundproof chambers. The chambers were artificially lighted to simulate perpetual summer. The warblers are summer residents in Europe, and had they been living in the wild they would have migrated in the fall to Africa. Although the warblers were isolated from any clues as to the approach of fall in Europe, they became restless as summer ended. They moved constantly about in their cages and stayed awake much of the night. If they had been allowed to migrate, they would have been awake at night while making the sojourn to Africa. As a matter of fact, according to Sauer, the birds' restlessness continued for about the length of time that it would have taken them to fly to Africa. After this the warblers settled down, appeared contented, and slept at night. But, again, when spring arrived in Europe, the birds became restless for the period of time it would have taken them to make the return trip. The warblers' biological clocks evidently were keeping time with an internal rhythm.

It has been found that robins can reset their biological clocks within a three-day period. According to biologist John D. Palmer, writing in the March 1966 issue of *Natural History*, the robins have an activity rhythm from sunrise to sunset and they sleep at night. If the birds are placed in a laboratory that is light at night and dark during daylight hours, the robins will adjust accordingly. Yet a caged robin can be placed in an isolated chamber with dim light intensity and temperature kept constant around the clock and the bird will maintain a pattern nearly identical to birds in natural settings.

Rhythmic activities cannot be explained in terms of the known principles of chemistry and physics. It has been shown that metabolic processes can be slowed or increased through the manipulation of temperature, but the tuning of the internal clocks appears to occur independent of temperature.

The immense distances traveled by the Arctic tern are amazing. This bird makes annual trips of around twenty-two thousand miles, between the Arctic and Antarctic regions, and yet will arrive in the Far North on June 15 and leave on August 25. The golden oriole arrives in the Northern Hemisphere six weeks before and departs six weeks after the summer solstice.

The remarkable timing of the swallows has brought fame to the Mission of San Juan Capistrano in California. The flock usually arrives at the mission from Central America on St. Joseph's Day, March 19. The residents of Medina, Ohio, claim that a flock of several dozen turkey buzzards arrive at nearby Hinckley Ridge on March 15 and have been doing so since 1810.

Another example of tight scheduling in migratory timing is the case of a bird known as the shearwater. During the course of a single evening in late November millions of shearwaters arrive on islands off Australia. This invasion is accomplished in less than half an hour, yet the birds converge from points as far removed as the North Pacific, the Bering Straits, Japan, and British Columbia.

In the October 1966 issue of *Scientific American*, Drs. John T. Emlen and Richard L. Penny relate their studies of penguins in Antarctica. The flightless birds travel hundreds of miles over what would appear to us to be featureless land and water. Emlen and Penny followed the course of the penguins for distances over a thousand miles and found that the creatures became somewhat confused on cloudy days but lined out straight courses on clear days. It was concluded that the birds were using the sun as a compass. In order to do this, however, it was necessary for them to allow for the sun's constant movement across the sky. Apparently, the penguins' biological clocks adjusted direction as the day progressed. The scientists explained that the clocks were able to reset themselves when the penguins were taken and released at new locations and at different seasons.

Apparently some birds use solar navigation but others do not, and studies have indicated that birds do not always use the same systems. Dr. Jean Dorst of the National Museum of Natural History in Paris stated in *The Migration of Birds*: "It is certain that birds do not use one particular sense, but that orientation involves many different phenomena that are difficult to distinguish."

It has been pointed out that neither bird nor man is able to move from one place to another with only the aid of a compass. Bicoordinate navigation necessitates the inclusion of the equivalent of a map by means of which the human or other animal can determine destination in relation to present position.

The Gaddises explained that most of the robins in this country return to within a five-mile radius of their northern home of the previous year. Other birds return year after year to the same trees after excursions of two thousand miles. The Alaskan curlew and the western Canadian golden plover fly thousands of miles over trackless seas to hit the small target of Hawaii. In 1931 a homing pigeon flew from Arras, France, to its home in Saigon, Vietnam, a distance of seven thousand two hundred miles.

Whatever theories we might propose to explain the navigational talents of birds and other animals, they must allow for the fact that homing pigeons have been put asleep, placed inside covered cages, and released at night and they have found their way home—in fact, having broken wings or being stripped of their feathers in a storm, they have walked home.

Dr. Lester Tarkington of the IBM Systems Research Institute believes that birds navigate by means of magnetic fields. Speaking at a meeting of the American Association for the Advancement of Science in Montreal, Canada, in 1964, Dr. Tarkington proposed that pectins in the eyes of birds enable them to detect differences in the gradient of the earth's magnetic field. He suggested that the structure and orientation of the pectin membrane make it an ideal miniature instrument for sensing an induced microvoltage. If this theory is correct, a bird searches for geomagnetic forces that generate a pattern of currents matching a set produced in flight near the gradient.

Most birds, reptiles, and some fish have pectins in their eyes, and the theory of geomagnetic navigation seems reasonable. However, the theory fails to explain how monarch butterflies can locate targets fifteen hundred miles away, how the green turtles navigate nearly fifteen hundred miles of open ocean to swim from Brazil to tiny Ascension Island, or how a cat can know the exact time of day.

Willy was a time-conscious cat. A great deal of the time he was nonchalant about schedules, wandering around at all hours, careless about when he ate. But Monday nights were different, according to Dr. Gustav Eckstein, a psychologist at the University of Cincinnati. In his book *Everyday Miracle*, Dr. Eckstein explained that Willy wanted his food promptly at seven-thirty on Monday evenings. Fifteen minutes later he would head down the block, pause at the stoplight, and walk several more blocks to a hospital. Once there he would perch on a windowsill and spend the next two hours watching a group of women playing Bingo in the nurses' dining room.

Dr. Eckstein followed Willy on three successive Monday nights. He wrote, "That cat knows Monday. That cat knows 7:45. I thought it might be food, but there was no food. Or a congregation of cats, but there were no cats. He was there at that exact time to hear and see women playing Bingo.''

In *Just a Mutt* Eldon Roark tells the story of Gyp, a German shepherd who was purchased when a pup by Herbert Neff of Knoxville, Tennessee.

After a second baby was born to the Neffs, Gyp wandered off and was not seen again for months. Then on Christmas Eve the Neffs heard a whine at the door and Gyp was back. He enjoyed all the festivities of the holiday, sitting near the Christmas tree, taking part in family activities, and getting his share of the turkey. The next day Gyp was gone again, but year after year he visited the Neffs at Christmas. They had no idea where he spent the remainder of the year or how he knew it was Christmas Eve but for ten straight years he never failed to appear.

When Gyp continued to appear year after year, a local newspaper began playing it up and hundreds of people across the country took an interest. They would call the Neffs and ask if Gyp had arrived. Many tried to track the German shepherd after he left the Neffs but no one succeeded until Gyp was eleven years old. A reporter for the *News-Sentinel* finally discovered that the dog had been living with an elderly man, J. R. Jones. He was not aware of the publicity surrounding his dog.

The following year Gyp failed to arrive at the Neffs on Christmas Eve. As he was getting old, the Neffs thought that maybe Gyp had decided not to make the trip. But late Christmas night he showed up at the Knoxville waterworks where Mr. Neff was superintendent. The night guards let him in. They fixed him a warm bed and Neff brought him some turkey. Neff thought it best that Gyp stay for another night in order to rest, as he was getting somewhat feeble. Gyp thought otherwise, scratched his way under a fence, and returned to old Mr. Jones.

As the months of that year passed Gyp became increasingly feeble. In November a grandson of Mr. Jones, on leave from his military base, spent Thanksgiving with his grandfather. Gyp followed him when he walked to the nearby railroad station. He never returned. On Christmas Eve and the following day the Neffs and dog lovers across the country hoped that the old dog might show, but Gyp and his mysterious built-in calendar had vanished.

Scientists J. Aschoff and J. Meyer-Lohmann set out to trace when, in the life of an animal, the biological clock starts ticking. According to Maurice Burton, in his book *The Sixth Sense of Animals*, Aschoff and Meyer-Lohmann placed domestic chicks, as soon as they hatched, in cages under constant conditions, so that there was no appearance of night and day. Temperature and humidity also were kept at a constant level. The movements of the chicks were feeble at first but as they gained strength a definite orderly rhythm became apparent. As movements increased from the third to the eleventh day a true circadian rhythm developed of slightly more than twenty-five hours.

Other rhythms than the circadian one can be detected even before the chick hatches. The chick must breathe quite some time before it hatches, and oxygen reaches it through the shell. F. Barnwell and L. Johnson measured the rate of this diffusion and discovered a distinct rhythm in the use of the oxygen. Despite the fact that the chick inside the shell cannot see, there was considerably more oxygen used during daylight hours than at night.

Part of the biological or internal rhythm appears to be of a chemical nature. At the December 1966 gathering of the American Association for the Advancement of Science, internationally respected biologist Dr. Britton Chance announced his discovery of a 160-second chemical cycle in cells that was keyed to twenty biochemical reactions involving the production of energy.

In addition to the biochemical factor, however, all living things have electrical fields. The force fields in organisms change in strength and polarity in response to both biological and cosmological occurrences. It has been found that voltage-change cycles correlate with phases of the moon and that peaks appear when the moon is new and when it is full. Daily voltages are brought to a peak in December when the sun is closest to the earth and to a low in summer.

Other cycles in addition to the solar and lunar ones are daily and semimonthly. The changes seem to be connected with fluctuations in the earth's magnetic field. For the most part, changes in the earth's field are caused by forces from outer space, including cosmic and gamma rays, and sunspot activity, as well as other electromagnetic waves that bombard the earth.

Scientists are constructing a picture of the manner in which physiological rhythms respond to environmental cues. Sometime the daily and yearly cycles "interwine to produce patterns of exquisite sensitivity that make an organism responsive to every nuance in its environment. This is as it should be. As parasites on the skin of our planet, we can be truly successful only when we become aware of its pulse and learn to pace our lives to the rhythm of its deep, untroubled breathing," Watson states.

"Our host, however, is not alone. Earth in its turn is ruffled by the galactic winds of change and subject to forces brought to bear on it by an even wider environment. Inevitably these forces filter through to us, and life on earth learns to dance to the rhythm of other bodies. The most insistent beat comes, naturally, from our nearest neighbors."

Elsewhere in *Supernature* Watson states, "We see living organisms as entities and tend to forget they are intricate societies of single cells and that each of the components has a great deal in common with all the other cells, not only in that individual but in every other organism that ever lived. Alexander Pope recognized that 'all are but parts of one stupendous whole, whose body nature is . . .' "

Whether we look to science, philosophy, or theology for our answers to life on this planet it no longer seems to matter. Within the various disciplines we find a common usage of such terms as "relatedness," "holistic," "unified," "synergy," "oneness," and so on, and a converging theory that all life exists in the pulsating sea of energy or consciousness.

"All of us who live are a part of the universal whole, fellow creatures in the cosmos, responding to the ceaseless ebb and flow of the universe," Vincent and Margaret Gaddis tell us. "And there are other voices from out of the deep that speak in languages still unknown to man."

7

The Prophets

It has been said that man makes a habit of ignoring the prophets in his midst. While this charge usually refers to our myopic approach to human seers, it can be equally applied to our treatment of animal savants. When prophets finally do win acceptance, we expect them to be the wisest among us, and it is a bit humiliating perhaps to discover that the "lower" members of the animal kingdom are informed on what's going on around us before we are.

Yet animals—respecting their own internal crystal balls—have saved thousands of human lives by indicating forthcoming earthquakes, avalanches, hurricanes, tidal waves, and other disasters. They have also performed seeming miracles as prophetic monitors of bombings, shellings, fires, and the demise of ships at sea. They do better than most of our meteorologists at predicting the weather and have served as psychic witnesses of events yet to occur in the human domain.

At Concepción, Chile, in 1835 at ten-thirty a.m. the sky was filled with seagulls constantly screaming. At eleven-thirty a.m., horses ran around in a panic knocking down fences, and the dogs rushed out of the houses and into open areas. At eleven-forty a.m. the town was leveled by an earthquake.

Just before the tremendous earthquake that shook Alaska in 1964, animals in zoos as far away as Seattle were reportedly behaving in an agitated fashion. Before shocks hit Chile and Peru, it was noticed that the seagulls abandoned the shoreline to fly many miles out to sea.

The August 26, 1963, issue of the Denver *Post* quoted Dr. Edgar W. Spencer, of Washington and Lee University, as stating that prior to the 1963 earthquake in southeastern Montana birds disappeared from the major quake area several hours before the first tremor was felt.

The March 24, 1969, *U.P.I. Report on Soviet Studies* reported that a Russian woman living in Tashkent claimed that her spitz dog saved her life in the Soviet earthquake of 1966. The dog dragged her outdoors and away from the house just a few minutes before the quake destroyed her home. A Tashkent schoolteacher said that ants picked up their pupae and migrated from their anthills about an hour before the first shock. At the Tashkent zoo the mountain goats and antelopes refused to enter their indoor pens quite some period before the quake, and days before the shock the tigers and other large cats started sleeping in the open.

Biologist Lyall Watson states in *Supernature*, "The Japanese, who live right on a fracture system, have always kept goldfish for this reason. When the fish begin to swim about in a frantic way, the owners rush out of doors in time to escape being trapped by falling masonry. The fish have the advantage of living in a medium that conducts vibrations well, but even animals living in the air are able to pick up warning signals. Hours before an earthquake, rabbits and deer have been seen running in terror from the epicenter zones . . ."

Animal sensitivity is one of the components in a current push by the People's Republic of China to establish an earthquake prediction system. According to Dale Mead, wrting in the March 1976 issue of *Science Digest,* a group of ten U.S. geologists and geophysicists recently visited China under the auspices of the National Academy of Sciences' Committee for Scholarly Communication with the People's Republic of China in order to learn more about their methods for predicting quakes. They learned that the Chinese were using electronic equipment, monitoring sounds coming from the earth and fluctuating water levels, and observing the strange behavior of animals.

China averages six quakes of at least 6.0 on the Richter scale each year, the highest in the world. Chinese methods of prediction have been so accurate, the visiting scientists reported, that they claim to have saved thousands of lives.

Mead stated in his article that the Chinese people were alerted to earthquake prediction methods employed by past generations. "The historical records said that farmers could tell that something was vastly wrong in the earth beneath them when normally placid horses reared and raced. Dogs howled. Fish leaped. Animals that were rarely seen, like snakes and rats, suddenly surged from their hiding places by the dozens . . . "

To test the Chinese animal-watching techniques in this country Dr. Barry Raleigh, of the U.S. Geological Survey's earthquake research facility at Menlo Park, California, visited Hollister County in California, a rural area prone to smaller quakes. He and a colleague, Dr. Jack Everndon, asked farmers and ranchers in the area if they had noticed animals behaving strangely before the November 1974 jolt. While a number questioned had not thought of observing animals, one woman told the scientists, according to Mead, that she had tried to calm two horses that were quite spooked for reasons then unknown. A colt ran around in such a frenzy, she said, that it fell down. Everndon discovered that the ranch stood almost directly over the center of the quake.

Dr. Everndon was told by a San Fernando official that two police units in separate areas reported seeing large numbers of rats scurrying in gutters the night before a major quake in 1971.

An earthquake destroyed more than three-fourths of Skopje, Yugoslavia, on July 26, 1963. It was reported that during the early-morning hours of that day the animals of the local zoo aroused the zookeepers from their sleep. Elephants charged the bars of their cages, tigers and other cats paced their cages and constantly roared, and two bloodhounds at the police station leaped at the windows in efforts to escape the building. Officers on patrol particularly noticed the absence of birds in the town.

Naturalist Ivan Sanderson contends that what is involved in animal prediction of earthquakes is more likely supersensory perception than what we usually think of as extrasensory perception. Referring to Sanderson's theories, Vincent and Margaret Gaddis state in *The Strange World of Animals and Pets*, "Such acute awareness may detect approaching hurricanes by water-level fluctuations or drops in barometric pressure. Slight sounds or a rise in temperature may herald avalanches. Volcanic eruptions and earthquakes may be preceded by greater tensions in the earth's magnetic field. Animals may respond to minor trembling and small foreshocks."

Sanderson once watched fiddler crabs by the thousands march inland from the coast of Honduras ahead of a hurricane. The march started twenty-four hours ahead of the storm. The coastal area was badly flooded but the fiddler crabs knew exactly how far to move inland to avoid the dangerous effects of the tidal wave.

The Bezymyanny volcano struck the Soviet Union during the winter of 1955—1956 but not a single bear was killed even though many lived in the vicinity of the volcano. According to Russian scientists, the bears interrupted their hibernation and found safer spots to await spring several days before the volcano's activity was first noted on instruments.

Nandor Fodor states in his *Encyclopedia of Psychic Science* that prior to the eruption of Martinique's Mount Pelée in 1902, the cattle became extremely restless and could not be managed, dogs howled continuously, snakes left the vicinty, and birds stopped singing and left the area.

The swift has long been respected as a weather prophet. Sometimes called the storm-swallow, rain-swallow, and thunderbird as a consequence of its successes, the bird has been known to predict storms by evacuating an area when the storm is more than 800 miles away.

A farm family living near Lawrence, Kansas, had a cat that predicted a tornado. The cat gave birth to four kittens in the barn. A few days later, however, the family noticed that one of the kittens was missing, and on subsequent days another kitten was discovered to be missing, until all of the kittens were gone from the barn. That night after the last kitten disappeared a tornado completely wiped out the barn. The mother cat and her kittens were reported to be safe and sound at a neighbor's house a few miles away. This place had not been touched by the storm.

Mrs. Freda Robinson of Oklahoma City watches her tomcat, Felix, rather than the local television stations for an accurate prediction of the weather. Felix for four years now always takes refuge in the top of the Robinson wardrobe when the weather is going to turn wet and stormy. On the other hand, if he settles down on the windowsill, sunny skies can be expected. Mrs. Robinson claims that Felix has never been wrong.

It is claimed that snakes in a zoo will invariably hide from human beings when rain is forthcoming. However, the traditional long-range weather forecaster is the groundhog. It seems that the groundhog always emerges from its place of hibernation on the same day each year—February 2. If the day is cloudy and he cannot see his shadow, then he will remain in the open. This allegedly means that the weather will be mild for the remainder of the winter. But if he pops back into his hole, don't pack your thermies— six weeks of frosty weather remain.

Gene Hereth of the U.S. Animal Research Trust has studied the results of groundhog forecasting for the past eighteen years and states that the creature has been accurate fifteen out of eighteen times.

Animals have not only been successful in precognitive monitoring of the weather and natural catastrophes but they have done well in foretelling imminent danger from man-made storms as well.

When England was being pounded almost nightly by the German Luftwaffe during World War II, many Englishmen learned to watch their cats for a signal that a bombing raid was forthcoming.

Before the approaching bombers were picked up on radar and the alert was sounded, cats were noticed to spring into action. The hair would stand up on their backs and they would race for the bomb shelters. Humans soon learned to quickly follow. Stories ran in the English newspapers and before the war ended the cats were awarded the Dickin Medal, engraved with the words, "We Also Serve."

An explosion of a different sort apparently was predicted by a cat that enjoyed sleeping on or beside a television set. Vesey-Fitzgerald, writing in the British *News of the World*, told of the cat, who it seems belonged to a friend. One day the cat jumped off the set, stared at it intently for a few seconds, and then demanded to be let outdoors. Thereafter whenever the set was on, the cat would leave the room. Several days later the picture tube exploded, blowing fragments of glass about the room.

In 1956 Ted and Dorothy Friend told in their column in the San Francisco *Call-Bulletin* of a woman with the unusual name of Welcome Lewis who was saved by the psychic premonition of her boxer. Mrs. Lewis brought her dog with her from Los Angeles while visiting in San Francisco. She took him to Lafayette Park for exercise, but the boxer refused to get out of the car. Instead he barked and raised quite a fuss. Finally Mrs. Lewis gave up and returned to her hotel. The dog did not hesitate to leave the car.

The following day she passed the same park and discovered that a huge tree had fallen on a car in the exact place where she had parked. She also learned that the tree had fallen only minutes after she had pulled away.

A heartwarming story of a dog protecting a woman he did not know is told by Louise Rucks in her April 24, 1976, column "Hound Hill," which runs in the *Oklahoman and Times*. It seems evident that the animal could foresee danger for the woman and therefore took steps to protect her. Mrs. Rucks quotes the letter:

"I enjoy your Hound Hill, and look forward to it every week. My main reason for writing you is to tell you of a queer experience I had with a large black dog while I was in Baltimore 15 years ago when my husband was in the Marine Hospital and had leukemia. This is a true story and actually happened to me.

"At that time there were many rapes and muggings going on in daylight as at night. My husband and I worried about my walking the three dark blocks from my rented room to the hospital.

"The second night this huge solid black dog stepped out of a hedge and all but scared me to death. He walked me to the hospital and waited until I went back to my room. He stayed down on the sidewalk, never taking his eyes off me, until I climbed the steps and opened the door to the house. I was in Baltimore for two weeks and each night that wonderful dog escorted me to and from the hospital and waited to see me safely in the house. How safe and relieved I felt!

"The last time I saw him was the day I had to leave for home. He escorted me to the hospital and back but did not show up that night as my husband was released and walked with me. I do not know where the dog came from or where he went nor how he knew I would not need him the night my husband was released. I do not know how or why he knew I needed him.

"I have wanted to tell you this for a long time. Ever since I found your Hound Hill in the Oklahoman. But it sounded so weird. I hesitated until I could stand it no more."

And Mrs. Rucks comments: "This letter didn't sound weird to me. I agree with Henry Beston, nature writer, who wrote that animals are not brethren or underlings. They are 'other nations, caught with ourselves in the net of life and time, fellow prisoners of the splendor and travail of the earth.' Fellow nations do sometimes come to another's aid."

Spotty, a dog of mixed blood but mostly German shepherd, also had a premonition that his presence was required to protect a woman from danger.

The July 1959 issue of *Fate* related that during the depression years of the 1930s Mrs. Maude S. Translin of Palo Alto, California, was working at Stanford University. Near her home was a hobo jungle, and it bothered her that she was alone until late at night. Then Spotty was given to her by a friend who was a policeman. The dog was intelligent and he understood that he was to serve as watchdog for his mistress after dark. During the day, however, he was allowed to go with her son to his job.

One summer afternoon Mrs. Translin arrived home from the university around five and was surprised to find Spotty waiting for her on the porch. This was the only time he had ever done this. Spotty entered the house and planted himself so that he could watch all entrances.

Mrs. Translin opened the house, including the doors, in order to cool it off and went into the bedroom to change clothes. Shortly she heard a loud rap at the front door. Frightened but not knowing what else to do, she called out, "I'll be right there." A rough man's voice growled an agreement. The next sound she heard was Spotty's toe-nails clicking across the floor and the man's voice calling out, "Will this dog bite?"

"Indeed he will! Just stand still," she responded. When Mrs. Translin emerged from her bedroom, she found Spotty standing at the front door, his throat rumbling and his teeth bared.

Her knees shook as she took hold of Spotty's collar. The caller was a huge, mean-looking man who snarled, "I'm hungry and I want a meal."

"I can't let go of the dog but if you will shut the door and wait, I'll bring you something out in the yard."

The task was completed and the man left, and Mrs. Translin sank to her knees and threw her arms around Spotty's neck. He had walked several miles through the heat to be with her several hours before her son would have driven him home in the car. This was the only time he had come home at that hour in the three years they had owned him.

The Gaddises tell the story of William H. Montgomery, who decided to fish for flounder off the coast of New England. He prepared his boat and then whistled for his setter Redsy. Always, since puppyhood, Redsy jumped at the invitation to go fishing.

But this day she refused to come aboard. Instead she stood on the dock and barked despite Montgomery's entreaties and sharp commands. There was no logical reason to believe that anything was wrong with the boat, and the weather that day was perfect, hardly a breeze and no clouds in the sky. More than fifty boats could be seen heading for the flounder banks.

Fortunately for Montgomery he trusted the intuition of his dog. He knew something had to be wrong, and if his setter wouldn't go with him, then he knew it was best to stay at the dock. Many of the boats that went out that afternoon never returned. With an hour of the time that Montgomery planned to set out the wind rose to a tremendous gale and an unexpected storm moved in from the sea. Huge waves, some forty feet in height, hammered boats and coastal cottages to kindling wood. More than six hundred lives were lost in the storm. It was the great hurricane of 1938.

Rats traditionally abandon a vessel at the dock before the ship sinks at sea. Such stories are supported by the experience of actor Raymond Massey and his wife. They told the story to Broadway columnist Danton Walker, who reported it in his book *Spooks Deluxe: Some Excursions into the Supernatural*.

During the 1940s the Masseys purchased a town house in Manhattan's East 80s. Across the street was a large brownstone mansion that was then unoccupied but later leased by a socially prominent woman and her family. She told the Masseys she could not get rid of the hordes of mice that inhabited the building.

A few days later, Mrs. Massey was astonished to witness a mass exodus of mice pouring from the brownstone house. The small creatures appeared panicky and confused. When a number of them scurried toward the Massey residence, Mrs. Massey called the exterminator. Several days later the socialite committed suicide.

The mansion stood empty for a time but was finally sold to a wealthy playboy. His death made front-page news, but before it did Mrs. Massey once again saw the mice leave the brownstone house in droves.

The next owner of the house was a prominent businessman. One morning while watering her plants in a window-box Mrs. Massey again witnessed the mice horde as it issued from the house across the street. A few days later the businessman while flying his own plane crashed in the Hudson River and drowned before he could be reached by rescuers.

Many stories are told of dogs predicting the impending death of their owners or someone close to them. A number of psychics allegedly predicted the assassination of Lincoln, but none more clearly than the president's dog.

The White House staff made every kind of unsuccessful attempt to quiet the dog when he suddenly went berserk. Although always so quiet and docile, shortly before the tragedy the animal raced around the house in a frenzy and kept up a dirge of unholy howling.

Thomas Hardy, the English novelist, had a wire-haired terrier as a close companion for thirteen years. The dog, named Wessex, showed a great liking for one of Hardy's friends, William Watkins. On a spring evening Watkins visited the Hardy home and Wessex rushed to meet him with excited barks. On this occasion, however, his excitement gave way to a piteous whine. Hardy thought that he had developed a sudden pain but investigation revealed nothing to be amiss.

Wessex joined Hardy and Watkins in the study. During the course of the evening, the terrier several times touched Watkins' sleeve with his paw and withdrew it with cries of distress. When Watkins left the Hardy home, he was in good spirits and seemed to be feeling fine.

Early the following morning the telephone rang. Wessex

had a habit of barking when this happened, but this time he remained silent. He lay on the floor with his nose between his paws. Watkins' son was calling to say that his father had died suddenly about an hour after leaving the Hardy home.

An ancient proverb states: "Know a grain of sand completely and you know the universe in its entirety."

It is enough of a struggle to allow that some observant souls among us can know what is happening a thousand miles away or what tomorrow will bring. But when other creatures than ourselves perform these feats, it challenges our belief systems if not our sanity. We can cope with this information in one of several ways.

We can deny the validity of such reports, which is easiest because no further demands will be made upon our conceptual structures or ideologies. A few doors are closed to us after that, but then we can always keep company with those who enjoy dogma more than truth.

We can allow that maybe such things do happen but, if so, that they are one of those mysteries we are sometimes confronted with, and since there is no way of understanding them the best thing for us to do is shake our heads at the wonder of it all and then turn on the TV set to something that won't put too much of a strain on our cerebrum.

We can allow that at least some animals have psychic sensitivity and can foresee the future, and can decide that the answers to such phenomena must reside in a more thorough examination of all kinds of nervous systems and brains. A courageous gesture, perhaps, and one entirely acceptable within scientific traditions, but one that may prove disappointing. Within contemporary synergistic views, the whole is more than the sum of its parts. Adding up the contributions made by each part of a system fails to provide us with a picture of how the whole behaves with its parts intact. One of the problems with most laboratory explorations is that the researcher manipulates the subject while expecting the subject to behave in its normal fashion. No experimenter can divorce his feelings and thoughts from his project, and these provide a nonmeasurable input. According to the latest findings in physics, feelings and thoughts produce energy and the experimenter becomes an unconscious part of the circuitry.

If we seek to understand how animals, or some animals at least, can be prophets, some help may be forthcoming through greater in-depth investigation of animals' supersenses. It has been learned that many creatures are more sensitive than we to subtle energy fields and vibrations. Because of this, they may pick up very slight variations in the environment and somehow recognize these as indicative of change. They react to these impending changes and we translate their behavior as prophecy. It would seem that the more civilized a people become the more they rely on technology to protect their survival and provide them with the things they want. For example, we no longer have to be sensitive to weather changes, for the local meteorologist will do this for us. The ability to distinguish between faint odors and slight sounds contributes very little to our survival.

Yet, man can reclaim the awareness of his senses when the occasion demands it. Writer Jim Phelan, who spent fourteen years in prison, wrote:

"The tyro in jail has not only to learn a new language and become adept in minor trickeries. He has to develop new senses, become animal-keen in a thousand ways not known to civilization. Long before the end of my second year I could tell one warder from another, in the dark and at a distance, by his breathing, by his scent, even by the tiny crackings of his joints. Presently I could smell a cigarette in another man's pocket six feet away, hear a lip-still mutter in church even while a trained warder missed every sound. From the way an official clears his throat a long-term prisoner will know whether that man is likely to report him for smoking an hour later—a long-sentence convict is not a person, he is an alert, efficient and predatory animal."

Many of the instruments we have come to rely on tell us of a universe all around us of which we are unaware without the assistance of the machine. Perhaps our fellow creatures, who have as yet failed to develop their own technology, are more aware of the worlds superimposed on each other.

But better eyesight, hearing, alert responses, etc., do not alone explain the nature of clairvoyance in people. Nor does the superior sensitivity of animals explain how a dog could know that his master was going to be assassinated, how mice could foresee the death a number of miles away of the owner of the property they were inhabiting, or how a dog would know to return to his house on a particular occasion in order to protect his mistress. Apparently something more than acute sensitivity is involved in such cases.

In an early chapter we discussed models of consciousness. If we can believe the new physics when it tells us that physical forms can be traced to energy fields and energy fields, in turn, disappear into consciousness, then the world is a thought. Its entire existence can be found in That which thinks it. All forms, all animals and ourselves included, in the final analysis exist as a thought. We have long believed that the ability to be conscious depended upon a certain structure and that the nature of this structure determined the degree of awareness. But the new physics tells us that the thought creates the form rather than the other way around.

This possibility offers us a different theoretical approach: The form or structure of a living unit may not always determine the extent or level of its consciousness. If, as the mystics have long contended, the brain is merely a piece of equipment used by the mind, then the mind may be aware, but if the brain is limited in its functions, then this awareness is inhibited—according to our standards—in its expression. Animals may in some ways be closer to the Universal Mind because they are not occupied so intently with the activities of the brain. They well may be projecting at all times a reflection of Universal Consciousness, in which time and space do not exist, but we, because of our own limitations, fail to compute it.

Space and time do not exist, we are told, in clairvoyant

visions. These highly talented persons tell us that their perceptions are not a product of the rational mind but of the intuitive mind. Because of this, their insights are difficult to translate to those relying principally upon logic and language. Perhaps this is not dissimilar to the problems faced by other creatures than ourselves.

8

Sensing the Supernatural

"On my travels out of the body I occasionally find myself in somebody's home. That may not have been my target but there I am. When this happens, I manage to sneak away as unobserved as I entered. I may see people in the house but only rarely do they see me, and usually these are young children who still believe in other worlds than just the physical one.

"But seldom can I slip in and slip out again if there is an animal present. Somehow their senses are more acute or sensitive and they see things that most humans do not. They look right at me and start raising a rumpus, and their owners will just tell them to be quiet since they don't see anything themselves."

We sat under the shade of an old cottonwood tree close to the water's edge. Even though it was early April a bright sun had warmed the afternoon air and the ten of us had decided to hold our workshop outdoors where we could laze on the new spring grass and give our thoughts greater freedom while listening to our most unusual workshop leader.

The occasion was the Interdisciplinary Conference on the Voluntary Control of Internal States of Awareness, sponsored by the Menninger Foundation and held at Council Grove, Kansas, on the shore of a lake. Ninety physical and behavioral scientists from this and several countries had been invited to the four-day conference. The afternoons were devoted to workshops, and on this particular day a number of us had chosen to meet with Robert Monroe. The topic of discussion: "Out-of-the-body experiences and their implications to the study of consciousness."

Perhaps more than anyone else Monroe is peculiarly qualified to discuss this subject, for he has logged more than a thousand trips where his awareness, or what is sometimes referred to as astral body, allegedly left his physical body and in full consciousness he allegedly traveled to other levels and realms. His experiences were described in his recent book, *Journeys Out of the Body*, and he has developed a rather intensive training program for stout-hearted souls who wish to garner the same experiences. More than five hundred persons from all walks of life—many of these psychiatrists, physicians, physicists, and other professional individuals—have completed the course, known as the Monroe Institute of Applied Sciences.

Several of us at the workshop, incidentally, agreed to participate in the training sessions during the fall of 1976. From having spent time with Monroe and having visited with several who have already "graduated" we feel comfortable with the thought that our horizons of reality are in for some expansion.

It is exciting to talk about Monroe's experiences, but, alas, that is not our task here. He is being mentioned here because he can give us a firsthand account of what it's like to be a "ghost" and to be seen or not be seen by those still grounded on this planet. And it is interesting to learn that with few exceptions—notably clairvoyants and non-programmed young children—animals are aware of his presence whereas humans are not.

We often assume that human perception is much keener than that of other animals and that we therefore understand more about our world than our less-endowed brothers. But if we can believe Monroe—and many of his observations have been verified by some of the country's leading experts—then we are faced with the strong possibility that many of our animal friends are aware of levels of life surrounding us on all sides that we know nothing of. We may think we understand our environment but we may observe only a fraction of its total substance.

Mark Twain once stated that when he was a teenager he was appalled at the ignorance of his father and was amazed a few years later at how much the old man had learned. When we arrive on our elevated plateaus of consciousness someday, we may discover that the least wasn't last.

Another friend of mine has had some experience as a dweller on two planets. While not as seasoned a traveler as Monroe, he recalls one space trip rather vividly when he spooked a whole neighborhood of dogs and felt badly when distraught owners started calling their pets all sorts of unkind names, never guessing that the pets were simply aware. It is interesting to note that in his experience animals were found living on "the other side." He said that he once again petted and loved an Airedale that had died several years before, and also made contact with deceased pets of family and friends. "You can't imagine how happy my dog was to see me again . . . it was really hard to leave him again."

Occasionally, Fred Kimball talks to animals who have passed away when requested to do so by the former owners. A representative case, he said, was a dog named Lamb. The dog told him that when he passed away he was quite old and suffering from a lame leg. Lamb told Kimball he wanted to die so he wouldn't be a bother to the family. "When I told the surviving family," he said, "they substantiated the dog's claim, saying that 'one day, Lamb just lay down and died.' "

Charles Rhoades, director of the New Age Center in Oklahoma City and an accomplished psychic, is frequently called upon to exorcise homes of unwanted spirits who hang around and irritate the physical inhabitants of the structure. He told me that in his experience animals are more sensitive to supernatural phenomena than humans. "If the pets in the home haven't and aren't reacting to some mysterious presence, then I have found that seldom or ever will I pick up anything. In such cases I am likely to assume that the spirits are the products of hallucination or vivid imagination."

"Animals often display uncanny sensitivity to environmental elements which humans ignore," Dennis V. Waite states in an article, "Do Animals Really Possess a Sixth Sense?" which appeared in the May 1975 issue of *Probe the Unknown*. "Often they seem aware of events and phenomena which people either do not perceive, or only dimly realize," Waite explains. "Reports of apparitions commonly involve awareness and fright of a pet before its owner realizes anything is amiss. Many times in the cases of UFO's, animals displayed intense fright."

Dr. Robert L. Morris, Research Coordinator of the Psychical Research Foundation, Durham, North Carolina, as well as research associate of the Gardner Murphy Research Institute of Chapel Hill, North Carolina, tells how one early psychic investigator routinely took his dog with him on his investigations as he felt the dog showed more responsiveness to psychic phenomena than humans.

The psychic power of animal totemism still exists in various parts of the world. The Gaddises tell how anthropologist Geoffrey Gorer and scholar Ronald Rose discovered that totems were vehicles for information that was believed to be acquired telepathically by Australian aborigines. The sudden appearance of the totem bird or animal announces to the member of this totem clan an accident, illness, or death of another member of the clan. Sometimes the animal is an apparition and sometimes the unusual behavior of the actual animal transmits the telepathic message.

The Gaddises also tell the story of Paul M. Vest of Santa Monica, California. His Chihuahua, Gringo, became seriously ill with a stomach and intestinal infection. Antibiotics were used but the dog got worse and the veterinarian gave up hope.

The dog was taken home too weak to eat, stand, or even lift his head. Vest sat in a chair that night holding the small dog, and he felt such great compassion that he thought, "Isn't there somewhere a power, a force that will help this suffering, dying dog?" As it was a question rather than a prayer he did not expect an answer, yet it had been a vivid concept with deep feeling.

Almost immediately, a strange scene unfolded. First, Gringo pricked up his ears as though hearing something and then slowly he raised his head and his eyes became fixed on something. Vest felt something strange and uncanny in the room. He followed the dog's line of vision and was shocked when he saw a small figure resembling a man but having a rather doglike head. He saw the figure for only a moment. "It definitely was there, a solid, three-dimensional object." Gringo apparently continued to see the figure after it disappeared from the man's vision and he reportedly seemed to be listening to sounds inaudible to Vest.

The dog's body was tense and trembling but in a few moments he looked up at his master with a different look in his eyes. He got slowly to his feet and wagged his tail. That night he drank warm milk, slept soundly, and in a few days was good as new.

What strange combination of a man and animal came from another dimension to intercede in the animal's behalf? How was the man able to call forth this help? Or was his appeal only coincidental with the figure's appearance? Why did the figure appear to be both human and doglike? Would it be reaching too far to assume that the entity had sufficient power to take on any desired form but chose one acceptable to both the man and the animal? Mythology is rampant with stories of persons half man and half animal and equipped with paranormal powers. Perhaps these myths are less fiction or symbolic than we have assumed. The force that manifests itself is not always one of a kind and loving nature, as when the black magician takes on the demihuman form of the werewolf.

The entity that visited Norma and Tom Kresgal one

night was entirely beneficent and quite well known. It was their long-dead pet collie Corky and they credit him with saving their lives.

Writing for the *National Enquirer*, Miss Nicole Lieberman, a member of the American Society for Psychical Research and longtime lecturer on psychic phenomena, told the story of the Kresgals and their miraculous escape from death.

It seems that Norma found the dog in 1946 under strange circumstances. She and Tom had recently been married and were living on a farm in New York State. A neighbor called and asked her to sit with his sick wife while he went to town for medicine. He returned in half an hour and Norma started walking home. After a short distance she experienced the sensation of not being alone. She stopped, looked around, saw nothing, and continued walking.

But the feeling persisted and for a reason she could not explain she felt compelled to leave the path and move into the forest. Fifty feet ahead she discovered a large collie lying stretched out with his neck red with blood.

He was still alive and wagged his tail feebly when she stroked his head. He was much too large for her to carry, so she rushed home for help. She and her husband's father took the dog to a veterinarian. The vet was able to remove a bullet from the collie's throat but there was permanent damage to the voice box and he was never able to bark in a normal way.

No one claimed the dog, and Norma named him Corky. He was her close companion for seven years. When he died, they buried him under a tree on the farm.

Two years later the Kresgals moved to New York City and into an upstairs apartment in a two-family house.

They had lived in the apartment only a few months "when I was suddenly awakened one night by a strange sound," Mrs. Kresgal told Miss Lieberman. "It was Corky's hoarse bark. I thought I was dreaming and was about to go back to sleep when I heard him again—loud and clear."

Norma got out of bed and opened the bedroom door. She was met by great clouds of smoke. She aroused Tom and they were able to get themselves and their landlord from the house before it was engulfed in flames.

"The tears were running down my face. Tom, thinking I was upset about our things being destroyed, told me not to worry because we were insured.

"He didn't know I cried in gratitude—thanking God with all my heart for letting my Corky come back to me long enough to arouse me—before it was too late."

The Arabs claim that horses are not to be matched for their prowess and sensitivity by other members of the animal kingdom. They claim that the horse is guided, particularly at night, by spirit forces.

Many horsemen besides the desert dwellers claim that a horse can sense the presence of spirits and ghosts and displays a marked reaction to psychic phenomena. In my youth I spent considerable time astride horses and I have had them suddenly stop as though sensing danger ahead. The reason was not always discovered and I feel certain now the horse was aware of something beyond the range of my senses. On one occasion late at night, however, the horse quite suddenly stopped in the middle of the road for no apparent reason. For about one minute she refused to move, and this was exasperating, as it was starting to rain and I was anxious to get home. Then she started trotting again but as she did so a bolt of lightning struck the road ahead of us—at a spot where we would likely have been had she not paused.

In *ESP with Plants and Animals* Beth Brown tells the story of an officer who was taking a load of sick and wounded persons out of back country with a wagon pulled by a single horse. It was in country which could not be traveled by car or truck.

A blizzard descended on them and the officer soon became hopelessly lost. In desperation he gave the horse free rein and resigned himself and his caravan of sick people to death. But the horse turned around, went a short distance, and turned again. On and on the horse went, plodding through rapidly growing drifts.

They entered a forest and crossed fields the driver did not recognize, and the falling snow covered their tracks as quickly as they were made. There was no longer any possibility of the horse guiding himself by scent. Yet some inner guidance allowed the horse to deliver his load safely in the courtyard of a hospital in snow that was falling and blowing so thick that the officer in charge could hardly see his hand in front of his face.

The spirits of horses have also been experienced after they are gone. There was the ghost horse of Angus McDougall, the sculptor, and his brother Ken, sons of the famous Dr. William McDougall, professor of psychology at Harvard for a number of years and director of the psychology department at Duke University at the time of his death in 1938.

When Angus was sixteen and Ken thirteen the family held a family picnic supper near an old deserted New England farmhouse located in the White Mountains. They were driven there by a Miss Baird, whose father owned the farm, in her Model T. The road, long-unused, was so rough, however, that they finished the journey on foot.

The ancient two-room house stood in the middle of an overgrown pasture atop a hill, a gaunt and desolate sight against the sky. The adults settled on a spot with a view some distance from the house and made preparations for the meal. The boys went ahead to explore the old abandoned structure.

The shingle roof was still intact but the only door hung inward by a broken hinge. Only an earth floor remained inside, but there was a stair leading to the attic. Ken climbed to the attic while Angus walked around to the back of the house.

"There several lank elderberry bushes had grown up over the roof forming a sort of tunnel or passage against the wall," Angus told a reporter years later. "I stepped inside this passage, and at once heard a horse snorting and kicking against the house." He thought at first that it was his brother playing a trick on him but Ken appeared from around a corner of the house. Together they heard the horse snorting and pawing. The sound was desperate and loud.

They went back into the house, but it was as empty as before. "We stood staring at one another in utter bewilderment. Ken turned very white in the face, and no doubt I did too. Without speaking we walked slowly back to rejoin the picnic party by the cliff."

Miss Baird was telling the sad history of the place when the boys arrived. Many years before, she said, the tenants to whom her father had rented the property decided to pull stakes and move west. They loaded all of their belongings in a single wagon. Left behind on the land was an old white horse that they believed would be too weak to make the journey.

Evidently the horse went into the house to seek shelter from a storm, the door swung closed, and it was trapped inside. Mr. Baird found the carcass of the old horse when he came out in the spring to inspect his property. He buried it under the earthen floor of the house.

A friend has a small log cabin away from it all in the high country of western Colorado. He uses the cabin several weeks during the summer months to put the finishing touches on whatever novel he happens to be working on at the time. The trail to his cabin is passable only by four-wheel-drive vehicles, but in years gone by there was a road used by miners, and later it served a logging operation.

One night while at the cabin alone he decided to wander through the nearby woods, as a full moon had cast a magic upon the tall and silent mountains. He was mesmerized by the breathtaking beauty surrounding him, and thoughts of how fortunate he was to be there instead of in the city passed lazily through his mind. But he was jarred from his reverie by the distinct sound of a horse's hooves pounding down the path toward him.

Not sure who might be horseback riding in those remote parts and at that hour of the night, he quickly stepped off the path and behind a large tree. The pounding of the hooves became louder, then they seemed to be directly in front of him, and then they slowly faded away down the trail.

He stepped from his hiding place, from which he had been able to see up and down the trail, and he was quite bewildered, for the horse was never seen. "The moonlight was so bright that one could even see the color of the grass," he told me, "and there was no way I could have missed seeing the horse as it passed . . . yet there was only the sound."

He heard the horse another time, about the same hour and on the same kind of night, but on this occasion he was too far from the trail to have seen the horse in any case. But one morning while a friend was visiting he was asked, "Does someone around here ride a horse on the trail?"

A little startled, he mumbled, "Well, I don't really know . . . I suppose riders do come up this way once in a while . . . Why?"

"I suppose I'm not used to the peace and the silence of this place. I woke up last night and couldn't get back to sleep so I pulled on my pants and boots and stepped outside. It was a beautiful night so I wandered out through the trees and damned if I didn't hear somebody on a horse coming down the trail like they only had a second to get where they were going."

"Did you get a look at them?" the host asked, coffee cup poised in midair waiting.

"No, and that's a funny thing. I thought I could see the trail but my view must have been blocked by trees or branches, because the sound was right there and then it sounded on down the trail and was gone, but I didn't see anything."

My friend didn't mention to his visitor his own experiences with the phantom horse, not knowing how it might be accepted.

Usually stories of ghost animals involve dogs, cats, and horses, possibly because these are the most common pets. Several years ago, however, while conducting a meditation retreat near Bear Creek Canyon in Colorado, I had the good fortune to see a phantom deer.

It should be explained that the site of this retreat was unusual in several ways. On the property are five of the largest blue spruces I have ever seen. They tower above all other trees in the area and are believed to be inhabited by a very high deva who watches over the property. Because of the presence of this spirit, it is known as a healing place and was known as such by the American Indians before the white man came.

Several of us go there at least once each year for a week or so to relax, meditate, and "get it back together again." We have had some unforgettable experiences and it is always a delight to share with the wildlife that abounds there—deer, porcupines, ground squirrels, chipmunks, gray squirrels, birds of many kinds, and even skunks, who come close because they know they are loved and will be protected. Several years ago we constructed a shrine of white quartz, from Bald Mountain, to St. Francis, the patron saint of animals. We are sure that the animals understand why we built the shrine.

One of the large spruces stands at the edge of the road through the property, and I have found this to be a particularly good place to meditate at night. Sitting with my back against the huge tree I experience contentment, peace, and distinctive high vibrations. On this occasion I had slipped outside alone after a lively philosophical discussion in front of the fireplace. It was a hauntingly beautiful night, full of stars and magic, and I decided to meditate on my special piece of earth.

I had not meditated for long when something made me open my eyes. Not twenty-five feet from me, walking slowly along the road, was a deer. At first I thought it might be the large buck I had encountered in the woods that day. I had come upon him in a small clearing. We looked at each other for a few moments, then he went on grazing while I passed on by not more than twenty feet from him.

But as the deer drew closer I realized it was much

smaller than the buck I had seen earlier. It seemed to be aware of my presence, for it paused on the path and seemed to be looking in my direction. When it stopped I was startled to find that I was looking at the deer but I was also looking through it. The doe appeared real enough except for the transparent quality of her body, for I could clearly see the shadowy bushes on the edge of the road directly through her.

I mentally asked her to come closer, but her only response was a momentary pause to look back in my direction as she continued unhurriedly up the path in the moonlight. A hundred or so feet up the road where I sat she turned into the woods and disappeared. I have not seen her since, and yet on another night beside the tree I felt a touch on my cheek that for all the world felt like the soft, chamois-like nose of a deer, but that was all, a touch, and nothing was to be seen.

They say that the "Dun Cow of Warwick" in England is definitely an apparition. Her hoofs are silent and she leaves no traces on the grass. She comes to warn the Earl of Warwick before a member of the family dies.

Two white owls alight on the roof of the manor house as a similar omen for the Warders of Arundel. And white birds of unidentified species have appeared, according to legends, on the Salisbury Plain whenever the Bishop of Salisbury is dying. They are said to be large birds that fly with unmoving wings of white dazzling brilliance.

The birds were seen in 1885 by Miss Anne Moberly above the Palace of Salisbury shortly before the death of her father, the bishop. Again, in 1911, according to Christine Hale, author of *Haunted England*, Miss Edith Olivier, who was unacquainted with the legend, was returning home from taking a boys' choir on their annual picnic. At dusk they saw two large white birds gliding over the meadows in the direction of Salisbury three miles away. All members of the group saw the birds and stated later they had never seen such birds before. On their arrival in Wilton they learned that the bishop had died that day.

The disappearance of a bird is an omen of death at Longleat, the estate of the Marquis of Bath. When the head of the estate is about to die, it is said that one of the swans takes flight from the estate's lake and never returns.

The present Lord Bath told author Hale that during World War I, when his elder brother, then the Marquis, was fighting in France, his mother saw a swan fly away as she stood by a window. Five swans flew toward her, then circled the mansion. One swan then turned out of the formation and flew into the distance while the four returned to the lake. The following morning she received the official telegram informing her of her son's death.

Paul Ghali, a reporter for the Chicago Daily News Service, wrote in a dispatch from Paris that was dated October 18, 1958, about an experience of a friend of his, a well-known diplomat. Visiting the diplomat at his home in Place Rue St. Florentin was a relative, a refugee from the 1956 Hungarian revolt.

She appeared distressed one morning and he asked her what was wrong.

"I heard that owl last night."

"Nonsense, what owl?"

"No nonsense, just like back home. In Hungary an owl comes and hoots at the bedroom windows each time a member or a very close friend of the family dies."

"Even if it weren't rank superstition," he scoffed, "it couldn't happen here. How could an owl get anywhere near your window? We are in the middle of the city. There are no trees to attract any kind of bird. Besides, I can't think of any relatives, here or back in Hungary, whose time is up."

But the following day at breakfast the diplomat wearily admitted, "Aunt Ergie, you were right. I heard the owl myself last night. What sinister hoots in the dark! It must have been perched on the roof of the American Talleyrand Hotel. A nuisance, to be sure, but I don't believe in your death omens."

Yet at lunchtime that day the telephone rang, bringing news that the wife of the diplomat's first cousin had been killed in a car wreck fifty miles outside Paris.

All life forms seem to be enveloped in singular consciousness, not separate, but each having knowledge and contact with one another at some level of being. The great collective unconscious becomes at times the conscious, and during these moments we are amazed at the threads that hold earth-beings together. Space and time disappear, life and death lose their distinctions, and all that remains is Oneness whispering to itself.

The English magazine *Prediction* several years ago told of a remarkable cat named Fingal. It seems Fingal had a highly developed sense of sympathy, responsibility, and affection for other pets. One pet was a turtle who had a habit of falling backward on his back and then was unable to struggle upright. When this occurred Fingal would run excitedly to some member of the family and insist on their effecting an immediate rescue.

The cat would stay close by the cage if one of the rabbits got sick, keeping vigil until the crisis had passed. But when a human got sick, Fingal would keep his distance until he or she was better. This was considered an omen by the family.

Fingal kept a regular schedule. According to his owner, Celia Dale, "He liked to go out in the evening, stay an hour, and return punctually at nine o'clock. Then he would tap loudly on the French window to be let in."

Shortly after Fingal died the tapping at the French window commenced again. It would be so insistent that they would open the window. The tapping would then cease. On several occasions they were convinced they heard purrs from Fingal's favorite yellow cushion.

One afternoon a friend of the family brought her Siamese cat along for a visit. When the cat approached the chair containing Fingal's yellow cushion, he arched his back in fright. His eyes seemed to follow something as it moved toward the window. When the window was opened, the visiting feline—apparently aware that the original occupant of the chair had left—settled down on the vacated cushion.

One cat continued to be seen by a number of people

many years after its death. The British writer Elliot O'Donnell relates the tale of the phantom cat in his book *Animal Ghosts*. The story was told to him by a Mrs. Louise Marlowe.

Shortly after the turn of the century Mrs. Marlowe was visiting a friend in the Yorkshire village of Congleton. One day while taking a ride in a pony cart they stopped near the ruins of an old abbey to pick wild roses. As the women approached the abbey gates they saw perched on top of a hedge post a large, magnificent white cat.

"I wonder if it would let us pet it," Mrs. Marlowe commented.

They approached the cat but it suddenly leaped into the air and disappeared. The women were bewildered, for the grass was cut too short to conceal the cat, but it was nowhere to be seen.

Two evenings later they drove down the same path and once again saw the white cat sitting regally on its post. The cat observed their approach with a friendly demeanor but as they drew close, the animal slowly faded away. They stopped for tea in the village and mentioned the case of the disappearing cat to a waitress. The only response was a knowing smile, but a woman at the next table asked if it had been a large white cat.

"Good gracious sakes!" she then remarked. "You drove by at the right times to see Congleton's ghost-cat!"

The woman went on to say that she had lived in the village more than fifty years and recalled the cat when it was living. It had belonged to a Mrs. Winge, a housekeeper at the abbey. She was devoted to her pet. One day the animal disappeared and she was certain it had fallen victim to a dog pack. She was surprised, then, to hear meowing at her door a short time later. Joyfully she ran to the door to let her pet inside, but no matter how much she coaxed he wouldn't enter.

The cat stood at her door for a time and then disappeared. At first she thought he was just flighty after his experiences, but the same scene happened night after night. Each night Mrs. Winge opened the door but the cat refused to come inside. Finally one night by bright moon-light the housekeeper saw her beloved pet simply dissolve away. Mrs. Winge was quite upset by the realization that her cat was now a ghost and she refused to answer its meowing at the door. Soon she left the neighborhood, telling friends that she liked live cats but she didn't enjoy being visited by a dead one.

The woman at the tea shop concluded her tale by saying that this had happened forty years before, but the sight of the ghost-cat remained a well-known phenomenon in the village.

In *The Book of Sunnybank* Albert Payson Terhune tells of Rex, his ghost collie. Rex was a huge crossbreed and from puppyhood he was completely devoted to Terhune. Rex's favorite and only resting place was a spot in the hallway outside his master's study. He was not allowed in the dining room but he would watch the family at meal-time through the french windows from the verandah be-hind his master's chair.

Rex died in 1916 and during the summer of 1917 a friend of Terhune's came, the Rev. Appleton Grannis, who had not visited Sunnybank for a number of years. One after-noon Terhune and Grannis were talking while seated at the dining-room table. Terhune's back was toward the french windows.

As they left the room the minister commented, "I thought I knew all of your dogs, but there's one I never saw until now. The big dog with the short fawn-colored coat and a scar across his nose. This dog has been stand-ing outside the window staring in at you all the time we've been in this room. He's gone now. Which of your dogs is he?"

Rex, who had been dead a year, was the only dog who fitted this description. Grannis, however, had never seen Rex when he was alive, nor had Terhune mentioned him.

Another friend of Terhune's, Henry A. Healy, had made a study of Rex, for he was involved in studies on the prob-lems of crossbreeding. One evening he and his wife called on the Terhunes. As they were leaving, Healy remarked,

"You know, Bert, I wish there were some creature so utterly devoted to me as Rex is to you. I've been watching him as he lay at your feet. He kept looking up into your face every minute with a queer kind of adoration."

"Good Lord, man! Rex has been dead for more than two years!"

Healy was upset by his failure to remember. He frowned and finally said, "Yes, I remember now," and he hesitated several seconds before adding, a little defiantly, "Just the same I would swear he was lying in the firelight at your feet all evening!"

Terhune noted that one of his Sunnybank collies, Bruce, lived for four years after Rex's death. He was the only dog at that time allowed in the study. During these years Bruce never crossed the stretch of hallway that had been Rex's resting place. When Bruce entered the study he very carefully detoured around this spot as though to avoid something lying there. This was witnessed, Terhune stated, by a number of guests.

The late Dr. Nandor Fodor, the famous psychoanalyst who was aclaimed for his contributions to parapsychology, told in his book *Between Two Worlds* of the experience of Mrs. Henry Wipperman of Howard Beach, Long Island, New York. Mrs. Wipperman had two dogs, Skippy and Teddy. Skippy died from asthma and was buried in the yard of the home. That same evening, Skippy's familiar and distinctive wheeze was heard in the house. Not only did it claim the attention of Mrs. Wipperman and her mother, but Teddy raised his ears and searched the house for his playmate.

Seven years later Teddy died. "I broke down crying and patted his head. He let out a long sigh," Mrs. Wipperman told Dr. Fodor. "The next day he was dead and we buried him. That evening I heard the special pant he developed when he became sick. I was embarrassed to mention it, but when I heard it again I asked mother, 'Did you hear him?' She said yes, she had heard him, but did not want to tell me lest it upset me."

Dr. Fodor explained that hallucination was not the answer in this case. Not only was Skippy's wheeze heard independently by both women, but by Teddy.

Sometimes it seems that pets return momentarily to this plane of life in order to perform a certain task. In their book *The Strange World of Animals and Pets* Vincent and Margaret Gaddis state that in 1940 Mrs. Ruth Whittlesey, the wife of a Protestant minister, was serving as superintendent of a convalescent hospital in Hawthorne, California.

In March of that year she was summoned to the hospital in the middle of the night to be with a patient who was dying. She was close enough to the hospital to walk but she had to cross a lonely area with no houses or street lights. As she moved from the lighted into the unlighted section a car containing two men pulled up alongside her. She started to run but the car followed her.

But at that moment Mrs. Whittlesey's huge white collie Nigel raced up and planted himself between her and the car. The men took one look at the dog and took off in a hurry. Nigel stayed with her until she reached a lighted area and then he was gone. As she recovered from her fright, it suddenly dawned on her that the big collie had died several months earlier. Mrs. Whittlesey wrote the Gaddises: "My husband is a minister of a well-known Protestant church. We are not superstitious or overly imaginative—but we know that sometimes God moves in mysterious ways."

"So above so below; so below so above" is an ancient adage. In our lack of knowledge we may place too much emphasis on the distinctions between life during and after death whereas life may be life whenever it takes place and the differences may be ones of observation than of wise perception. Today we are witnessing a complete reassessment of the human potential and are allowing for far vaster possibilities of growth and accomplishment than we dared imagine even a few years ago. Would we equate this expanded inner universe with a single life form, the human, and imagine that it alone moves toward some far-off but accessible goal?

Perhaps we should remember a prayer first uttered by St. Basil, Bishop of Caesarea, in A.D. 370:

"O God, enlarge within us the sense of fellowship with all living things, our little brothers to whom Thou has given this earth as their home in common with us.

"May we realize that they live not for us alone, but for themselves and for Thee, and that they love the sweetness of life even as we, and serve Thee better in their place than we in ours."

9

The Imprisoned Splendor

I watched as he walked by the large diamondback rattler. It showed no tension, nor did it coil. Yet two steps forward by myself and the deadly snake instantly snapped into a coiled, fighting position. I quickly backed away. The Indian smiled. "You are not his brother," he said.

"He smells fear in me," I replied.

"Yes, but he reads your heart," my companion said. Rattlesnakes abound in the great Southwest, but Indians are seldom numbered among their victims.

The snake may be one of the most underrated members of the animal kingdom. Snakes do not have fins but they can swim as fast as many fish. While they do not have legs, they can travel as fast as a man. Some snakes can climb a tree as ably as a monkey, but they have no hands or feet for the climb. They sleep without closing their eyes and can detect sound, although they do not have complete ears with which to hear. Snakes crawl upon the ground and yet are among the cleanest of all animals. Perhaps in our aversion to the snake we should examine our own inadequacies rather than what is wrong with the snake.

"When you look at a snake and call it loathsome, are

you not speaking of a condition within yourself?'' my Indian friend asked. ''Look at what the snake has to work with—no hands, no feet—and yet he does very well. Do you resent this in him?''

Why do so many people shrink at the sight of a snake? According to Genesis, man was tricked by the serpent and therefore would always despise him, but this does not offer us a very plausible explanation for man's behavior toward the snake. It may explain how the writer of the first book of the Bible felt toward snakes, but snakes have not always been treated so badly by other cultures than the Judeo-Christian ones.

The American Indian does not respond in this manner, nor does the East Indian, who accepts the supernatural wisdom of the snake and the coiled serpent as the symbol of universal energy. The ancient Egyptian held snakes in high esteem and believed them to possess psychic powers that could bring good fortune to those who cared for them. The pharaohs often kept large collections of snakes, feeding and pampering them. They used the snake as a symbol of protection, and the serpent with its tail in its mouth was a symbol of infinity and the oneness of life.

In ancient Greece the snake was held in reverence. It was believed that snakes had the power to heal. Both Greek and Roman gods of medicine were depicted holding a staff with a snake coiled around it. Mercury, the messenger of the gods, is usually shown carrying a winged staff, called a caduceus, and twin snakes are coiled about it. This is the symbol of the medical profession.

A god named Kukulcan was worshipped by the Mayan Indians of Yucatan. He was represented as a large serpent with a feathered tail and protected the entrance to the temple.

The Hopi Indians of New Mexico and Arizona continue to use the snake in their annual religious ceremonies. They do not worship the snakes but rather believe that the creatures, being highly psychic, carry messages to the higher spirits. The snakes are collected by Hopi men and boys and are placed in earthenware jars. During the ceremonies Indian priests dance with the snakes in their hands and even hold them with their mouths. Treated with respect and kindness, the snakes never attack their human handlers.

Beth Brown notes in *ESP with Plants and Animals*: "It is a well-known fact that although a rattlesnake will attack a white man, it will seldom strike an Indian . . . No war exists between the rattler and the Indian. They live at peace with each other. An Indian can walk in safety close to a snake without any fear of attack."

What happens when a white man and a snake meet? Equipped with the Judeo-Christian belief that snakes are loathsome and to be despised, the man recoils, and as the adrenaline starts to flow something intensely savage within him makes him want to kill the snake. The snake may be a completely harmless garden variety, actually performing worthwhile deeds of exterminating insects and field mice, but the man is driven to exterminate it. His mind is inflamed with hatred and this poison radiates through his vibrations and thought-waves.

The snake is highly sensitive to these energy fields, and the man's emotional and mental attack places him on the defensive. He, in turn, is affected by these fields and his alarm system directs him to either flee or strike back. If he strikes, it is because he has been given no choice. "Rattlers do not strike when unprovoked, and even when encroached upon, they lie quiet, hoping to escape detection," according to *American Wild Life*, published by William H. Wise and Co., in 1954. "Finally, when there is no alternative, the frightened reptiles make a stand . . ."

"Watch a real American Indian walk into the vicinity of this same rattlesnake, you would witness something entirely different," J. Allen Boone notes in *Kinship with All Life*. "For one thing you would be unable to detect the least sign of fear or hostility in either one. As they came fairly close, you would see them pause, calmly contemplate each other for a few minutes in the friendliest of fashion, then move on their respective ways again, each attending strictly to his own business and extending the same privilege to the other. During that pause between them they were in understanding communication with each other, like a big and small ship at sea exchanging friendly messages.''

I have close friends in the tribes of the Cherokees, the Sioux, and the Crow. They have told me of the strange psychic exchanges between the Indian and nature, of how to listen to the message in the wind, how to find oneness with the heart of the coyote.

When in college I spent some time during the summers following the wheat harvests from Kansas, through Nebraska, the Dakotas, and into Canada. I worked for a while in the grain and cattle ranch country of South Dakota and became acquainted with an Indian girl, Lois Flying Cloud, a full-blooded Sioux. Ours was not a romantic attachment as such but more a brother-sister relationship. In any case, we became extremely close although the time spent together was not long. Sometimes I would see her in the evening after coming in from the fields. She served as the secretary for one of the churches and was saving her money to study art. As she frequently worked in the evenings, I would sit in her office and read until she finished. Then we would go some place to talk. But Sunday was our day together, a picnic lunch, and a hike into the hills, and the magic of discovery.

Lois was fortunate. She had been raised in an Indian family that understood the need to cope with the white man's culture. Yet they valued highly the mystical insights of their people. These they passed along to their children, and Lois Flying Cloud was a mystic.

Listen carefully to the wind, for it brushes the soul of all living things. Some small particle of everything it touches is borne with it on its travels. Scents, pollen, dust, yes, but much more than these, for there are whispers of sound that change ever so faintly by the arrangement of that which is passed by the wind."

She would have me close my eyes and taking my hand would lead me to various places and I was to tell what surrounded us—trees, rocks, hills, grass—by the sound of the wind. I would sit and with eyes closed was to point in her direction as she moved in a circle about me some hundred feet away. Occasionally I was right and when she rejoined me we would laugh about the problems of getting a white man "in tune." When our roles were reversed and I would lead her about, she seemed to be more aware with eyes closed than I with mine open. "There is a large bird passing overhead," she said. I looked up to see a hawk gliding in the sky above us.

Later lying on the grass, lazily gazing up into the sky, I asked her, "How did you know the bird was there, Lois? You couldn't have heard it."

She didn't answer for a while. She rolled over and gazed into the grass as though watching some occurrence. Then slowly, "As me, Lois, I could not see or hear the hawk, something apart and not of me. But, then, I release myself and I am no longer locked in this body. I reach out and all that was not me becomes me . . . words are difficult . . ." She ran her fingers through the grass, caressing it as though it was the hair of a loved one.

"When my spirit flies it rides the wind, becoming one with all that is, and I am no longer a girl seeing a hawk and I am just as much a hawk seeing a girl. Where do I end and the flying bird begin? I do not know . . . I only know he is part of my existence. He is there. I see him in myself. Perhaps you would say that the hawk and I communicate telepathically. This may be, but I speak to the hill and the grass, and the hawk knows these, too, and we are all one, breathing and being breathed by the Great Wind."

A number of years later, remembering Lois, I was to write in *Let Me Do This Thing*, a book-length poem:

Let me permeate
this embryo within the shell
becoming eagle life,
approach the world
from some high precipice
to sing the song of freedom
in my valley sweeps
and winged mountain climbs.
Let me chase the hare,
be the hare chased;
know the mastery of the hunt
and know the pain,
the terror of the hunted;
know not to take
what I have not given;
nor seek out
that which I have not offered.
Let me prey on the jungle
that I might eat
and offer myself
as that same sacrifice.
Let me traverse the air
I have spun;
navigate the water
flowing in my arteries;
grow in the soil
drawn from my own being;
feed on the grass
I have sown and nurtured.
Let me eat of the flesh
on the altar
built of myself
and when I would sleep,
let it be in the nest
of twigs torn from my limbs
and of matter dug
from my substance.

Let me do this thing
for I would sing
and echo myself
across a thousand hills,
rising as vantage points,
that I might see the expanse
of my own being.
I would play with the seeds
for my sowing
and eat of the harvest
gleaned of my increment.
I would cry to the night sky
full of the stars
flung from me
to the outer reaches of myself.

I am God becoming me;
this is the dream I would dream.

Lois taught me that the Indian moves the best that he can in conscious rhythm with what he calls the Great Spirit, the Unified Consciousness of all that is. All life forms are to be respected and loved as part of oneself, and this is not done only in the philosophical sense of sharing life upon this planet, but in the belief that in an ultimate sense there is no separation.

This sense of oneness reaches its highest manifestation in the Indian medicine man. His training, longer and more intensive than that required for any graduate degree offered by our culture, is not completed until he can overcome the limitation of subject-object perception.

Speaking to ninety leading scientists of this and several other countries at the Interdisciplinary Conference on Voluntary Control of Internal States several years ago, Rolling Thunder, chief medicine man of the Shoshone Indian Nation, said that the medicine man must learn complete oneness with all forms of life.

"How can he understand life if he is not part of it?" Rolling Thunder said. "He must learn to live in the heart of the coyote. This is not a poetic gesture of imagining what the wolf or the owl feels; the medicine man must direct his consciousness within the animal and understand himself as a bird, a coyote, and so on. He must actually see through the eyes of the coyote, hear through its ears, to think its thoughts . . ."

This amazing ability of the human to learn from animals about the world usually assumed to be beyond their level of understanding is not limited, of course, to any particular group of people. It is a state of awareness that can be gained by anyone who is patient enough to listen to life.

Boone tells of finding this quality in a man who spent his life in the desert in company with animals. He states in *Kinship with All Life* that Mojave Dan "was the only human I had ever personally known who could carry on silent two-way conversations with animals and really share ideas with them. Dan never reads books, magazines or newspapers, never listens to the radio, never watches television and seldom asks questions of other humans; yet he is amazingly well-informed at all times about practically everything that interests him, either nearby or afar. This information comes from his dogs and burros, from wild animals, from snakes, from insects, from birds, indeed from almost everything that crosses his trail. The real mystery was not so much Dan's ability silently to communicate his thoughts to the animal but his capacity to understand when the animal spoke to him."

True understanding of life, according to Rolling Thunder, operates from a point within the mind itself, where there is understanding of oneness between what is Self and non-Self. This oneness assumes that nothing interposes between them. There is no memory, association, choice, or discursive thinking about the object. If one can experience such a thing in its nakedness, apart from any properties attributed to it, he can experience oneness with the object and the subject-object arrangement loses its significance. The undifferentiated vision is what awakens one to spiritual awareness, the medicine man said. "This awareness is out of space and time, it has passed beyond both.

"With one's mind, one can reach toward an object and discover an identity. But the identification does not need to be made for it is experienced by the removal or stilling of that which intervenes between the two. Unity is experienced through being."

One finds considerable similarity between the words of an American Indian medicine man and those of a man trained in the wisdoms of the Orient. Dastur ("Dastur" designating a Zoroastrian High Priest) Framroze A. Bode has stated: "The Supreme Reality which is the ultimate and the irreducible is a Consciousness pure and undifferentiated. It is the 'chit' which is one and universal everywhere—the Spirit Divine. This consciousness is a creative force which manifests itself as a sovereign power. All creation is an emanation of this Consciousness. The Being is 'Sat'—Absolute Existence; 'chit'—pure Consciousness—and their common essence is 'Ananda'—Bliss. There must first be the pure changeless source Consciousness from which must flow the 'tattvas' or principles of creation which, in their manifestations, become the changing active aspects of the Cosmic Consciousness. In all states of consciousness there is but one supreme unitary underlying experience which can reach the state of subjective illumination. When this pure Consciousness is dimly refracted into ego-consciousness the beginning of dichotomy is experienced. When the unit of consciousness is diffused and the source is hidden, this bewildered limited consciousness is called 'maya,' and further fragmentation ensues in the multiplicity of creation. Life is a continuous process of distillation from the diffusion of Cosmic Consciousness. Consciousness distills wisdom from the experiences of the complexities of life." Dr. Bode serves on the faculty of the California Institute of Asian Studies, San Francisco.

And I can hear another Indian medicine man, Mad Bear of the Iroquois, saying that what we think of as consciousness is only the mental range of the human and that there is much that is invisible, inaudible, and intangible to most men. "There are ranges of consciousness," he told me, "that most people have no contact with, but unconsciousness is simply another level of consciousness. Unconsciousness does not exist in the universe. Consciousness can be found in the animal, the plant, the atom, in everything of nature. We are not fully awake if we do not experience consciousness in nature."

It would seem that the more awake or enlightened the individual the more his realization that consciousness permeates life itself and not merely one of its forms. Ramakrishna, Patanjali, Jesus, Buddha, Mohammed, Wesley, Schweitzer, Black Elk, Einstein are just a few of the world's great minds who could communiate and learn from all kinds of animals in addition to the human one.

"It is from understanding that power comes; and the power in the ceremony was in understanding what it meant; for nothing can live well except in a manner that is suited to the way the sacred Power of the World lives and moves," Black Elk states in *Black Elk Speaks*, the classic by John G. Neihardt.

Black Elk has had a vision and he makes it clear that a man who has a vision is not able to use the power of it until after he has performed the vision on earth for the people to see. Part of the vision had to do with gaining the powers of the bison and the eagle and much care was taken in designing a ritual that would manifest these powers. At one point in the ceremony Fox Belly chanted the following words:

"Revealing this, they walk.
A sacred herb-revealing it, they walk.
Revealing this, they walk.
The sacred life of bison—revealing it, they walk.
Revealing this, they walk.
A sacred eagle feather—revealing it, they walk.

Revealing them, they walk.
The eagle and the bison—like relatives they walk.''

Don Juan, the Yaqui shaman, makes it quite clear to
his student, Carlos Castaneda, that in order to understand
the teachings he must gain knowledge of the spirit inhabiting the body of the animal. "It was not a dog! How
many times do I have to tell you that? This is the only
way to understand it. It's the only way! It was 'he' who
played with you," he insists in *The Teachings of Don-
Juan: A Yaqui Way of Knowledge.*

Lois reached out her hand and the red squirrel took
the piece of bread from her fingers. It did not scamper
away. It sat on its haunches close to her and nibbled away
at the food. We had eaten our picnic lunch that day in a
cottonwood grove bordering the edge of a small meadow
creek. I had noticed an odd-looking bush some distance
away and had gone to inspect it. As I returned I saw Lois
feeding the squirrel and I waited until the small creature
despaired of begging any more food and departed before
I approached.

"You've made a friend," I said.

"Oh, yes, but he gave more than he took."

"Do you mean in friendship?"

"That, too, yes, but he offered me food in return."
She read the puzzled look on my face and added, "Before he came to me for the bread he nibbled on the leaves
of that plant. It is a type of nettle and he was telling me
that it could provide food for me."

I thought about this for a moment and asked, "Have
you ever tested a plant offered by an animal?"

There was no hesitation. "Oh, yes, often. They
wouldn't tell me this if it weren't so. The Indian has
learned of most of his foods and medicines from the animals."

According to Indian traditions, the Great Spirit guides
the animals to the right plants to cure their ills. As naturalist Archibald Rutledge has noted, Indians learned the
basics of medicine by observing which plants were se-

lected by animals when sick or wounded. Chimpanzees and apes will stop the flow of blood from a wound by using packings of astringent leaves. Bears cover their wounds with hemlock or spruce resin, and a muskrat uses hemlock gum, which will not dissolve in water. Woodchucks have been observed to apply a splint of clay to a broken leg, usually reinforcing the clay with some fiber.

Birds and small creatures relish the fruit of bearberry honeysuckle, and the Indians of Alaska and British Columbia include this fruit in their diet. The Indians discovered from animals that the fruit is particularly useful when a laxative is in order. Animals that seem to be anemic or depleted in some way have been observed eating the flowers and fruit of the bull thistle, and this is to be found in the pharmacology of the Hopi and Navajo Indians. Older members of animal herds, suffering from bad teeth and gums, along with rheumatism, eat the leaves and stems of the common cowparsnip, and this plant is recommended to the elderly of several Indian tribes.

The Iroquois consider the snakeroot to have great mystical power. They learned of this power by watching the mongoose or weasel. This small creature, before attacking a snake, fortifies itself and boosts its courage with the leaves of the snakeroot. If the mongoose is wounded in combat with the snake, it will find a snakeroot plant, nibble some leaves, rest a bit, and once it has regained its strength, renew the attack.

Watching animals rub themselves against the leaves of the western yarrow on unusually hot days, the Zuni Indians found that rubbing the leaves of this plant on the skin would prevent sunstroke and alleviate heat rash.

Stomach and digestive problems are handled by several animals, including dogs and cats, by eating several mouthfuls of green grass. Female birds need lime to form eggshells and will fly to locales where shellfish are to be found. Buck deer, needing lime for horn growth, will seek out phosphate dredges where the water is rich in lime.

"There is beauty and wisdom in the squirrel, the moth, the raven, all of the creatures with whom we share the earth. But what are they or us but an expression of the Great Spirit? What we really see as marvelous is the Universal Being expressing a fox or expressing a lynx . . ." Lois Flyng Cloud ran a hand through her long black hair; it caught a ray of sunlight racing through the leaves and sparkled black diamonds—a young classic face cast in half shadow, struggling with an inheritance that demanded sharing.

"We become enchanted with the form of the horse or of the owl and imagine that they are limited in their intelligence and being and forget that they are only expressions of the All Knowing. Would we limit It? If this small creature is the Great Spirit expressing Himself, why do we not listen? Why do we imagine that God would create all manner of living things out of the substance of His being and yet limit Himself to existing within the human? How could He manage that? How could the All Knowing care for the hawk when He created him and care for him soaring in the sky, but not care when his body lies no longer moving on the ground? Why would He do that?"

I had sat down on the grass beside her and was staring away to the hills, listening, probing. "There are many mysteries we do not understand," I offered.

"Mysteries, yes, there will always be these, Bill, but would there be fewer if we were to find that all of these creatures exist within and not outside of us?"

A silence fell between us, not as a break but as a bond, and saying more than words. We remained until the first fireflies signaled the passing of the day. Hand in hand we made our way from the cottonwood grove, across the meadow, past the buffalo wallows, and up the cattle trail to town.

"I'll bet if they put their minds to it some of our four-footed friends could come up with some tests to prove they are more intelligent than we are," Lois said as we reached the last stretch of our journey. She giggled and then we laughed and it was almost all right that our day was ending.

10

Immortal Cry

Raymond and Suzanne Peters were exhausted. They had stayed up late several nights that week finishing their income-tax report and the night before had been up to the wee hours with a child with an upset stomach. Their bed was a welcome haven and their heads had hardly touched the pillows before they were sound asleep.

But they were not allowed to remain there. Sometime around three a.m. Raymond became vaguely aware of a dog barking in the room. Suddenly it was close to his face and so loud that in spite of their exhaustion both Raymond and Suzanne sat upright in bed.

"My God, Mac, what in the world is the matter with you?" Raymond asked of his Scottie. But in that same moment the Peterses became aware of the smoke filling the room. They rushed to the hall and it was filled with dense choking smoke. The far end of the hall and the ceiling were aflame. The fire had not yet reached the children's bedroom and they gathered the two small still-sleeping youngsters in their arms and fled down the stairs.

Their exit was none too soon, for the fire had already spread through the kitchen and the lower floor was quickly becoming a furnace. A next-door neighbor had awakened moments before and called the fire station. Although every effort was made to save it, it was too late and the house was a total loss.

Did Mac, the Scottie, also escape? In a way Mac had made his exit three months before when he died at the age of eleven from what was believed to be a weak heart.

Late one night I was also awakened from a deep sleep by the persistent barking of our dachshund, Phagen. I listened for a few minutes, hoping he would stop and I wouldn't have to go outside and scold him. The barking continued, sharp and quite insistent, so I pulled on a robe and slippers and made my way to his pen. He was not outside. I looked inside his doghouse with my flashlight and there he lay. He had been dead for several hours, as the body was frozen stiff.

But Phagen was to bark again. For two nights exactly at the same hour I heard him barking. Both nights I went outside. The first night I saw nothing but an empty pen and house. But the second night as I approached his pen in the semi-darkness of a waning moon I saw him in the shadows, waiting, and as I drew closer I saw him wag his tail. Awed, bewildered, I reached toward him . . . but in that moment he was gone. He never barked again. Was he just telling us farewell? Had he come back that night for a final goodbye? Was I stumbling out of my dreams and passing headlong into hallucinations? One might ponder this question except that my neighbor, who was not aware that our dog had died, asked me the morning following my final experience if something was wrong with Phagen as he had barked so much the night before.

Do animals have souls? Does something remain after death? What claim, if any, can they make on immortality? There is a general assumption in our culture that only humans are blessed with souls and immortal life, that once an animal's brief span is spent upon the earth he is gone forever except as his memory lingers on in the hearts of those who loved him. But that general assumption is far from unanimous among those who have been close to animals. It would be difficult today to convince the Peterses that a dog's being ends at the grave.

It would be equally difficult to convince my friend Robin Deland, of Denver, Colorado, that animal immortality is a myth. He was driving late one night on a narrow and winding mountain road. Quite suddenly in the road ahead of him appeared his large collie, Jeff, who had died one year before. The markings were unmistakable. Wide-eyed, Deland braked to a stop. He jumped out of the car, and, although his knees were shaky, he ran toward his dog, calling his name. The dog turned and moved slowly ahead of him up to the peak of the incline just ahead. As Deland reached the incline he saw a huge boulder in the road, deposited by a landslide. He would not have been able to see the boulder until too late. Either hitting the boulder or trying to swerve out of its way would have likely sent him over the cliff. He looked around for his former companion but he was nowhere to be found.

If animals do survive bodily death, what awaits them on the other side? As regards the human experience, there is a growing acceptance of the theory of reincarnation, which holds, in essence, that human entities return time and again to physical existence in order to learn and to grow toward perfection. To many observers of animal qualities such as love, loyalty, dedication, and sacrifice it is not acceptable to believe that these virtues are temporarily expressed and then are forever lost. The question then becomes whether animals can experience reincarnation and thereby evolve toward higher states of awareness. If they do not, how do we explain great intelligence and even wisdom in some creatures and not in others, just as with human beings? How did they arrive at these states, and what lasting purpose would be served by these qualities?

Few scholars today place much stock in the idea of the transmigration of souls, the theory that bestial humans may come back in animal form. Whereas there may be minor retrogressions within the human realm, most reincarnationists do not believe that humans revert to the animal kingdom. Nature, rather, appears to move from lower to higher states.

For those who find the reincarnation principle itself logically and inferentially acceptable, it is difficult to contend that only one class of life is moving purposefully upward and that all other forms of life are mere props to the human drama, as Dr. Cerminara questions in *Many Lives, Many Loves*. "All other classes of life do seem to participate in a dynamic evolutionary process, and there are a great number of structural and biological similarities between the various kingdoms. It is far more logical," she states, "therefore, to infer that there is one far-off divine event, as Tennyson put it, toward which the whole creation moves."

According to most traditions that accept reincarnation, it is affirmed as a universal principle, applying not only to human beings but to all life forms and centers of consciousness. Life is seen as coming from the Universal Source and all life is traveling, according to these teachings, on a long evolutionary journey back to that Source. "Broadly speaking," Dr. Cerminara states, "life evolves from the mineral kingdom to the plant, from the plant to the animal, from the animal to the human, and from the human to the near-divine and then the divine."

In *The Rosicrucian Cosmo-Conception* Max Heindel even goes so far as to say that the lower animals now on earth will at a later period "be a purer, better type of humanity than we are now . . ."

It should be noted, however, that most traditions consider that evolution unfolds for the human race as a whole but that individuals can break out of this cycle and through their expression of free will move at a faster clip. Following this line of thought, then, it seems reasonable to me to envision a certain animal species as moving along life's journey toward fulfillment at a certain pace, but with certain members of this species—possibly as a result of new experiences—moving ahead of the pack. We say that man to some extent creates his own destiny through an act of will. We have not endowed animals other than ourselves with free will, but the acts, behavior, intelligence, and evidence of choice demonstrated by many unusual animals—some exhibiting qualities superior to some humans—face us with possible reassessment of this theory. Is a dog who clearly demonstrates reason and makes choices as a result of this reason any less an individual than many humans who behave and believe according to the dictates of the herd?

The evidence for reincarnation of the human species is supported by the memories of individuals in waking consciousness of past experiences which can be tested and documented. The work of such persons as Dr. Ian Stevenson, head of the Department of Neurology and Psychiatry of the School of Medicine of the University of Virginia, has come a long way in recent years in supplying data that can be thoroughly checked and substantiated. This data consists primarily of cases of remembered past lives that are of recent enough origin that persons involved in those memories are still alive and can confirm the information.

Unfortunately, our inability to communicate adequately with other animals prohibits us from exploring such matters with them. This does not prevent us, however, from examining the evidence of life after death of animals. Whereas we may be able only to theorize what happens to animal consciousness after it leaves this realm, we can explore the evidence for life beyond the animal grave. If this adventure offends us, it is likely because our egos are attracted by the long-held belief in our privileged state. These theories were propounded, incidentally, by humans and do not necessarily reflect the opinions of other inhabitants of the kingdom.

Dr. Robert A. Bradley, a practicing physician in Denver and a pioneer in psychosomatic medicine and medical hypnosis, supports the idea that death does not end it all for animals. In his book *Psychic Phenomena*, written with his wife, Dorothy, he relates a personal experience with immortality:

"There is controversial discussion regarding the survival of animals after death. Our family does not question this premise since further evidence of survival after death came from a rather unexpected source. One of our dogs was a tiny two-pound Chinuahua who when let outdoors in the winter, would shortly bark his piercing, shrill bark to be let back in. He hated the outdoors summer or winter and would make himself irritatingly obnoxious until let back in.

"It was just before Christmas. The winter weather had set in. The family was busily making holiday preparations and on this night was involved primarily in trimming the tree. We hadn't noticed that the little dog had been let out (he had not barked to be let in) until one of the children noticed that he was missing.

"A search for the dog was started immediately by the children, but to no avail. We all then joined in the search both indoors and out, because I had the definite feeling something was wrong with the dog. We systematically searched and called outside the house and, not finding him, began a systematic search inside.

"Dorothy and Sieg remained at the Christmas tree, continuing to decorate. As the search party came to this hall where the tree was, Dorothy and Sieg were surprised to hear us all worriedly wondering where the dog could be. They assured us they had heard his series of shrill barks just before we came and supposed we had found him. We asked them, 'Which direction did the barking sounds come from?' They both seemed confused and pointed vaguely up toward the center hall, somewhere. I immediately said, 'He's dead. That was an astral bark you heard! He's met something unfamiliar and is giving his usual hostile reaction.' I had the sudden conviction we would find him dead. I got a flashlight and carefully explored the dark corners outside the house, and sure enough, there he was, frozen to death, just outside the window within a few feet from where Sieg and Dorothy were working trimming the tree. Fifteen to twenty minutes before on our first search I had stood practically at that spot and tapped on that window to ask Sieg to turn on the outside lights. I must have been within inches of the dog at that time but he was in a shadow where I couldn't see him. However, he was of a vivacious nature and had he then been alive would have made himself known.

"Examination showed his tongue and throat to be frozen solid, his jaws frozen shut. How was it possible for Dorothy and Sieg to have heard his series of vivacious shrill barks just a few minutes before? And, why were the sounds they heard coming from the opposite direction and from 'on high'?"

It is not uncommon for animals to be present in mystical experiences, and persons who have had out-of-body experiences report seeing animals on the so-called astral plane. In some instances they allegedly have been briefly reunited with a dead pet or have seen animals that others have identified as being their former pets.

A friend who has had a number of out-of-body experiences told me, "On one occasion I clearly saw Ben, my old collie who had died several months before. He was beside himself to see me, wagging his tail and jumping up against me. I petted him, talked to him, and never doubted the reality of the experience."

Mrs. Lowanda Cady of Wichita can thank her deceased dog for getting rid of a burglar. She lives in an apartment complex and several of the apartments in her section were being entered, although it was primarily food from refrigerators that was being taken. Late one night she was aroused from a deep sleep by the agitated barking of her dog, Jock. There were hurried footsteps in the rooms below her, a door was opened, and then sounds of someone running, accompanied by the barking Jock. Mrs. Cady investigated and discovered that an intruder had been helping himself to the contents of her refrigerator. She started to look for Jock and stopped, having temporarily forgotten in the excitement that her pet had died three months before.

In *The Strange World of Animals and Pets*, Vincent and Margaret Gaddis tell the story of Freda Aston of Tulsa Oklahoma, and a family dog, Fife, an English mastiff. When Freda was a young girl, the dog was badly mauled in a fight. His wounds were treated and he appeared to be recovering, but one morning he could not be found. The family was greatly concerned that the dog, then fifteen years old, might be lying helpless somewhere.

Then Miss Aston's mother had a dream in which she had a vision of Fife standing strong and proud in his prime. She saw him standing on a hill, happily wagging his tail. Then the dog looked down at his feet, and her eyes followed his and beneath him on the ground lay the battle-scarred body of Fife stretched out in death.

The following morning her mother took Freda by the hand. "Come," she was quoted as saying, "we are going to find Fife." She told the child about her dream and they walked to a place closely resembling the scene, a group of hillocks, that she had seen in her vision. "There lay the old body that had housed Fife's brave, loyal heart for so many years, just as she had seen it in her dreams," Miss Aston wrote the authors.

Sir Rider Haggard, famous British novelist who wrote *She* and *King Solomon's Mines*, had an unusual experience of dreaming about the death of a pet. His report on this experience and his signed affidavit appeared in the *Proceedings* of the British Society for Psychical Research in October 1904.

Shortly after midnight on July 10, 1904, Haggard cried out in his sleep, and he started struggling and gasping for breath. His wife awakened him and he told her that the dream had started with a sense of depression, and then he seemed to be struggling for his life. As the dream became more vivid, he sensed that he was trapped inside the body of his black retriever named Bob. "I saw Bob lying on his side among brushwood by water," he reported. "My own personality seemed to be arising in some mysterious manner from the body of the dog, who lifted up his head at an unnatural angle against my face. Bob was trying to speak to me, and not being able to make himself understood by sounds, transmitted to my mind in an undefined fashion the knowledge that he was dying." Haggard told his wife that he had a vision of a marshy area near their place.

Four days later Sir Haggard found the dog's body about

a mile from the house. It was floating in the Waverly River. It was discovered that the dog had been badly injured. A veterinarian stated that the skull had been fractured and the two front legs broken, and that it was likely the body had been in the water more than three days, probably since the night of July 9.

Haggard learned from two section hands that the dog had likely been struck by a train. They showed Haggard a spot near a trestle bridge where there was dried blood and part of a dog's collar that they had found on Monday, July 11. Later that day they said they saw the dog's body floating below the bridge. It was determined that the dog was likely struck on the trestle bridge by a freight train from Harlesdon at about the time of Haggard's dream.

We may assume that animals do not understand the nature of death. While they may miss a mate after it's gone or grieve in the absence of a departed owner, we may dismiss this behavior as not reflective of any insight into the meaning of death. But how can we explain an animal's awareness of death occurring to its master many miles away if it had no comprehension of its meaning?

Also puzzling are those cases where animals have come to pay their last respects and even have willfully given up life at the same time or shortly thereafter.

The September 1956 issue of *Fate* told a story of a bird lover named William Milburn who lived in Durham, England. During his life he had kept many wild birds, but during his waning years only one bird remained, a song thrush. She refused to fly away and burst into song whenever the old man appeared on the scene and sometimes would perch on his shoulders or head.

Milburn became ill with influenza and the thrush sang very little. On the day the man died and for the three days that his coffin was in the house the bird did not sing at all. Yet as the pallbearers raised the casket to take it from the house, the thrush began to sing, and she sang her heart out in a requiem as the procession moved away. When the hearse left for the cemetery, she was silent again, for she, too, was dead.

The June 1946 edition of the *Reader's Digest* tells the story of a small mongrel puppy that was adopted by the Seabees in the Gilbert Islands. She was fed canned milk through an eyedropper until large enough to eat on her own. Her foster parents, the crew of an LCT, named her Puddles and spoiled her as only lonely people do.

But the time came when the LCT had served its time. Orders came for it to be junked and sent to the bottom. Another crew attempted to adopt Puddles, but she refused, and regulations prohibited her from being taken to the States. Aboard another craft, Puddles only whined and refused to eat, so the crew allowed her to go back and watch as the condemned craft was salvaged of equipment. Sadly from the beach she watched as the men stripped the craft and finally towed it out to sea to be sunk. When the men returned to the beach after sinking the vessel, Puddles was still there, but she was watching no longer, for she was dead.

The Gambill Wild Goose Reservation near Paris, Texas, was named for its founder, John Gambill. Gambill once nursed a wounded gander back to health and the following autumn the gander returned with twelve geese that became quite tame, according to Joe F. Combs, feature writer for the Beaumont, Texas, *Enterprise*.

The next year the number of geese was in excess of a hundred, and by the time Gambill died in 1962 it was estimated that more than three thousand geese wintered in safety on the reservation. As Gambill died in a Paris hospital, hundreds of geese from the reservation flew into Paris and circled around and around the hospital, honking their requiem. Somehow, some way they knew.

What does death represent to an animal? At this point in time perhaps we have no way of knowing. Perhaps, as with people, it is an individual thing to be met by different animals in their own fashion. Some animals seem to be unaware of its approach, while some make preparations for the event; for example, certain dogs and cats search for places to be alone at the time of death, knowing that it is imminent.

Researchers have found that chimpanzees demonstrate a haunting fear of death. Citing the experiments of Dr. Adrian Kortlandt in the Congo jungle, Vitus B. Droscher states in *The Friendly Beast*: "We will recall the chimpanzee's fear of death expressed in his drawing back from dead animals, from the arm or leg of a member of his own species, even from sleeping animals and lifeless images. Such fear is of an utterly different nature from the fears manifested by other animals . . . But whether chimpanzees with this degree of consciousness of death are ever compelled to suicide, no one can say at present . . . It may also be that chimpanzees have a much stronger fear of death than men and for this reason alone are incapable of suicide. To the superficial view, the anthropoid ape's fright reaction at the sight of a corpse is certainly far more violent than ours. In this sense these animals evidently see the situation far more realistically than a man entangled in delusions and emotional confusions who wants to take his own life."

Dr. Kortlandt once placed a stuffed leopard with a realistic chimpanzee doll in its mouth on a trail frequented by a chimpanzee troop. After their fear and horror at the sight, they pounded the leopard to pieces with sticks, and then mourned the death of what they understood to be a member of their species. Dr. Kortlandt tells of this in personal correspondence with Droscher:

"At the first light of dawn the chimpanzee troop returned. In funereal silence they all assembled in a wide circle around the doll. Slowly, a few of them ventured closer. Finally, a mother with her baby clinging to her abdomen stepped forward out of the silent circle. Cautiously, she approached the 'victim' and sniffed at it. Then she turned to the assembled horde and shook her head. Thereafter each ape silently departed. Only one chimpanzee crippled by polio (strangely, these apes also suffer severely from infantile paralysis) remained for a while sitting beside the 'corpse,' looking steadily at it. It was as though he could not take leave of the face of death.

"Finally he too went away. After that there was a sustained silence. All morning long we did not hear a single chimpanzee cry, nor did we later in the day.

"But the high point of my whole expedition had been that chimpanzee female's shaking her head after gazing at the dead body. Of course we do not know what the animal wished to communicate to the silent onlookers. Perhaps it meant: 'No, unfortunately no sign of life.' But more probably it was: 'No, not any one of us.' We are equally ignorant of why that somber mood descended upon all the members of the troop. But an unexpected world always lies hidden behind these chimpanzee faces."

In her article "Magic Zoology in the British Isles," published in *Tomorrow* magazine, Summer 1953, Mrs. Grace N. Isaacs tells a story of a man named Henry who owned a large cattle ranch near Trelawney. He cared a great deal for his animals and would not turn their care over to others. He died unexpectedly and his coffin was placed in a wagon for the journey to the church and cemetery. The distance from the house to the gate of the estate was great and along this route a large number of mourners were gathered. During the procession the mourners were suddenly startled by the moaning and bellowing of cattle. Herds of animals gathered from the surrounding pastures and stood in long lines along the fence bordering the drive. They tossed their heads, pawed the ground, and lamented in tones quite unlike their usual lowing.

"Telling the bees" was an ancient custom of letting the bees know when their beekeeper had died. Sometimes the bee hive was drapped in black crepe. Following the custom of telling the bees, when Sam Rogers, a cobbler and postman of the Shropshire village of Myddle, England, died, his children walked around his fourteen hives and told his bees. According to the Associated Press, April 1961, the relatives of Rogers gathered at his grave and shortly after they arrived thousands of bees from Rogers' hives more than a mile away came and settled on and about the coffin. The bees entirely ignored the flowering trees nearby. They stayed for approximately half an hour and then returned to the hives.

A cat paid his respect at the grave of his master according to a story in the Autumn 1963 issue of *Tomorrow*, an English magazine. The correspondent stated that his grandfather and a cat named Bill were extremely close. The cat followed him by day and slept in his bed at night. The man was seriously hurt in a railway accident and for a week lay in a hospital several miles from his home. He died in the hospital and his body was taken from there to the church and then to the churchyard for burial. As the rites were finished, an uncle of the writer looked up and saw Bill approaching the grave. He moved with dignity to the grave, stood for a short time looking at the coffin, and having paid his respects, turned and headed home.

I used to delight in Albert Payson Terhune's stories of his Sunnybank collies, and I recall Jean, who, contrary to most animal mothers, paid special attention to one of her puppies long after he was grown. She brought him the tastiest bits from her dish, took him bones, and even though he was larger than she, she daily washed him from his head to the tip of his tail. Wherever Jock went, Jean was not far behind.

Then Jock got distemper and had to be isolated. This was before the days of antibiotics and despite the struggle by Jock to survive and Terhune to save him, the big collie died. During Jock's quarantine, Jean refused to eat.

Jock was buried in a field more than a quarter of a mile away. The following morning Jean was released and immediately she started searching every inch of ground, searching for her "puppy" and occasionally giving a sharp little bark that had always brought him running.

Finally she raced back for Terhune, her tail wagging. She caught hold of his coat and pulled him along to the mound that was Jock's grave. Jean lay down on the mound, her tail still wagging, knowing that Jock was close. Every day until her death years later, regardless of the weather, Jean visited Jock's grave, often staying for hours.

"Her waiting had no grief in it," Terhune explained. "It was full of gay hope."

Mr. and Mrs. Robert King, their small daughter, Mrs.

King's elderly father, and a cat named Felix lived in the small town of St. Kilda in Australia. The old gentleman died at the age of ninety and the cat couldn't be consoled. It roamed the house and yard, searching and crying. They decided to take the cat for a ride in the hopes of distracting him.

Felix was quiet until they reached the outskirts of Melbourne, when suddenly the hair on his back bristled, he trembled, and he leaped through the car window and disappeared from sight in the traffic.

There was nothing the family could do but return home and hope that Felix would find his way on his own. The days passed and Felix didn't return. Then Mrs. King and her daughter visited the cemetery with some flowers and there pacing back and forth on top of the grave was Felix. The cat was highly joyful at seeing them and started playing with the little girl as she had with the grandfather. The cemetery was ten miles from their home and more than five miles from where Felix had leaped from the car.

Twice the Kings tried to take Felix home, but each time they got him as far as the cemetery gate the cat leaped from the car and scampered back to the grave. They made arrangements with the custodian of the cemetery to feed and care for the cat.

When John Hetherington interviewed the family for *195 Cat Tales*, he drove out to the cemetery and there was Felix fixed like a sentry atop the grave. Hetherington wrote, "This story haunts me. Perhaps it's because there are in it features that lie beyond the frontiers of human understanding."

"We can hardly expect to find certainties in this nebulous realm," Vincent and Margaret Gaddis tell us. "Perhaps it is not so important what we believe as that we believe something and keep testing our beliefs. But upon one conviction we stand—that man cannot assign a surviving soul to himself, and deny it to his animal brothers; that both man and animal are creatures of instinct and reason with the difference one of degree and not of kind;

and that if consciousness does survive, it is a quality of life itself and not of homo sapiens.''

We need to reassess our relationship to life itself, to understand that if man's life is extended beyond a single chapter, then it is inconsistent to imagine that only the human spirit can seek fulfillment. With such a limited perspective, how would we understand J. Allen Boone's experience with the great dog Strongheart?

''Strongheart became the 'professor,' I was the 'entire student body,' and wherever we happened to be, either indoors or out, became our 'classroom,' '' Boone stated. ''That is how the curriculum functioned as long as Strongheart's physical body was bouncing around in the earth scene. And that is how it still functions. He is still my teacher, and I am still his pupil. Through the illusory mists of time and even death itself, he continues to share with me, through the eternity of goodness, things that are exceedingly important for me to know and to practice.''

Tennyson seemed to be convinced of the eternality of all of life when he penned the words:

> That nothing walks with aimless feet,
> That not one life shall be destroyed
> Or cast as rubbish to the void
> When God hath made the pile complete.

Theologians such as Martin Luther, John Keble, and John Wesly seemed to share this conviction. Speaking of immortality, Wesly wrote: ''The whole brute creation will then, undoubtedly, be restored, not only to the vigor, strength and swiftness which they had at their creation, but to a far higher degree of each than they ever enjoyed . . . as a recompense for what they once suffered . . . they shall enjoy happiness suited to their tastes, without alloy, without interruption and without end.''

Civilized man living in large cities has lost contact with nature and has become alienated from the animal kingdom. Yet, our alienation is also an ideological one, and this can be largely attributed to our theology. It may be

that in order to support the idea of man's "special creation" the early church fathers decreed that animals do not
have souls. Yet, this is a philosophy not to be found anywhere in the Bible, including the words of Jesus, and for
which there is no scientific proof. As a matter of fact, we
find in Job 12:7-10:

"But ask now the beasts, and they shall teach thee; and
the fowls of the air, and they shall tell thee:

"Or speak to the earth, and it shall teach thee: and the
fishes of the sea shall declare unto thee.

"Who knoweth not in all these that the hand of the Lord
hath wrought this?

"In whose hand is the soul of every living thing, and
the breath of all mankind."

We have been led to believe that animals were created
for man's convenience and pleasure and have no rights
whatsoever of their own.

Eastern philosophies have afforded greater attention to
the essential unity of all that lives, and the scriptures have
not been suppressed to meet the demands of an egocentric
theology. Mohammed taught, "There is no beast on earth,
nor bird which flieth with its wings, but the same is a
people like unto you." And Buddha said, "One thing only
do I teach: suffering and the cease of suffering. Kindness
to all living creatures is the true religion."

In recent years one of the greatest defenders of animals
was Albert Schweitzer. His life work was dedicated to the
philosophy that love has to transcend narrow ethical systems and that reverence for all life must be at the center
of our behavior.

Jane Dunlap, in her book *Exploring Inner Space*, says
that her mystical experiences " . . . left me with another
unshakable conviction . . . it is that all plants, animals,
and humans alike have much the same feelings you and I
have. For the first time in my life I became aware of a
wonderful oneness existing between all living things,
whether plant, animal, or human."

This is a state of awareness that appears common to
illumined persons throughout history, the conviction of the

oneness of life. Sri Ramakrishna drew the anger of the Brahmin priests when he took offerings of food placed on the altar for the Divine Mother and gave them to a hungry cat. St. Francis always referred to the animals surrounding him as his little brothers and sisters.

Speaking in *Many Lives, Many Loves* of her personal beliefs regarding animals, Dr. Cerminara said: "Yet I do not apologize for my sense of certainty. The certainty is this: Animals are related to us much more closely than we think. Though they lack speech, their mental processes are not very unlike our own. They are similar to us in their fears, their pains, their affections, their frustrations, their terrors, their devotions, their gratitudes, in short, in all their emotions, even though they may know them in lesser complexity and degree than we. They are, as Mohammed said, a people like ourselves. Regarded from the evolutionist and reincarnationist point of view, they must be a people struggling along like ourselves, on the long, difficult road to perfection."

11

Beyond Explanation

Few dogs have been called upon to help a larger number of people than was Rags. She was the only inhabitant of Sing Sing Prison who was there by choice.

Rags turned herself in at the gray somber walls during a cold autumn day in 1929. She served twelve years and became a legend in her own time. A small mongrel, part Scottie and part wire-haired terrier, Rags spent her days cheering up the dismal atmosphere of the prison. She worked out a set of tricks, stunts, mimicry, and acrobatics to entertain the men. A large part of each day was spent making the rounds of the shops, the cell blocks, and the hospital.

Rags befriended them all but was careful never to show partiality to anyone. She completely ignored the guards, the warden, and visitors. She would eat at a different table in the mess hall each day, systematically rotating in order not to miss a table. She left the prison compound at the end of the day to sleep in the warden's home but would return in the evening if there was going to be entertainment or a performance, never failing to know when this would be. Warden Lawes ordered the guards to let her in and out of the locked gates whenever she wished.

Rags was particularly sensitive to a despondent, brooding prisoner. She would rub her head against him, perform all kinds of acts to cheer him up, and then lead him to a group so he would not be alone.

One night Rags did not leave the cell blocks. She followed one of the prisoners to his cell and remained in front of it until morning. The prisoner had been refused a pardon and, discouraged, he had decided that no one cared what happened to him. He was determined to end it all that night by hanging himself with his bed sheet.

Rags never gave the man that chance. Every time he tried to slip out of his bunk, the dog would growl and he knew if he went any farther Rags would bark and bring the guard on the run. He finally decided that at least Rags cared what happened to him and he would give himself another chance.

Hobo, on the other hand, was dedicated to living up to his name. Hobo first appeared in 1957 at the railroad yards at Hopewell, Virginia. He first rode with switch engines but soon graduated to longer hauls. Over the years he traveled thousands of miles and, according to Doug Storer, author of *Amazing but True Animals*, was seen by train crews as far south as Tampa and as far west as Cincinnati. For the most part Hobo rode the rails of the Seaboard and the Norfolk and Western lines, in good weather riding the catwalks and when the weather was bad curled up inside the cab. Regardless of how far afield his travels took him he always returned to the Hopewell freight yards.

But Owney holds the honor of being "the most traveled dog in history," according to the U.S. Post Office. The story begins in 1888 in Albany, New York, when a small puppy slipped into the post office out of the cold and fell asleep behind some mail sacks.

Owney was fed by sympathetic postal clerks and for a time he devoted himself to learning the routines of the office. But watching the mail sacks being loaded into the railway cars must have sparked his wanderlust, for he disappeared from Albany for several weeks. Upon his return, the postal clerks fixed him up with a collar, identification, and a tag asking postal clerks to stamp the names of the places where Owney appeared.

Eldon Roark states in *Just a Mutt* that Owney traveled all over the United States and the number of tags attached to his collar was legend. The postmaster general presented him with a lifetime pass on any U.S. mail car and a harness to relieve the weight of the tags on his collar.

Owney went to Alaska in 1895, and conimg down the Pacific Coast he stopped off at Tacoma. He followed the mail bags up the gangplank of the S. S. *Victoria*, bound for the Far East. In Japan he was presented to the mikado, who decorated him and presented him with an honorary passport bearing the seal of the empire. Similar presentations were made by the emperor of China. His voyage around the world took him through the Suez Canal into the Mediterranean and across the Atlantic Ocean. By the time he arrived home he had accumulated two hundred medals.

When Owney died, allegedly as the result of a dog fight, his body was mounted and together with his harness and medals was displayed for many years in the Postal Museum in Washington, D.C.

Vincent and Margaret Gaddis tell the story of Spot in *The Strange World of Animals and Pets*. Spot was dedicated to his life as a fire dog. The mascot of Headquarters Company Station in Camden, New Jersey, he rode the firetrucks and watched the battles against raging fires.

One night, however, Spot changed his sleeping quarters from the fire station to the home of Mrs. Anna Souders, the widowed mother of his two young playmates, eleven-year-old Nora and eight-year-old Maxwell. The Souders home was across the street from the fire station.

A short time after making the switch, Spot was awakened by smoke. He rushed around the house barking a frantic warning, then he threw his weight against the door of Mrs. Souders' bedroom. Spot ran to the bed and pulled the blankets from the sleeping Mrs. Souders. She roused her children, flung open a window, and called for help. She then collapsed, unconscious, but Spot remained at the window barking. His barking attracted the attention of a patrolman, and all members of the family were rescued in time. Spot refused to leave the house until the children and Mrs. Souders were safe.

Jack, the Dalmatian mascot of Engine Company 105 of Brooklyn, New York, received the Medal of Valor from the Humane Society of New York. One day the fire truck on which Jack was riding wheeled out of the station in pursuit of a fire. Suddenly a three-year-old child dashed in front of the truck. The driver slammed on his brakes but the weight and momentum of the truck was too great. Jack leaped to the pavement, shot in front of the truck and rolled the boy out of the way just in the nick of time.

Another Jack, this one a baboon, was dedicated to the service of his master, James Wide, a signalman at the Uitenhage Tower on the Johannesburg-Pretoria Railway in South Africa. Wide lost both his legs in an accident but managed to carry on with the help of his pet. They lived together in a small cottage and had a garden. Jack did much of the work, pumping and hauling the water from the well, cleaning the house, watering and weeding the garden.

In Elsie Hix's *Strange as It Seems* she tells how each morning after breakfast Jack locked the house and pushed Wide to work in a small carriage. Jack won his real fame, however, for his ability to operate the levers in the railway tower. He knew every one of the various block system signals, and as the trains passed, he pushed or pulled the levers that set the signals. Further, when required, he operated the tower controls that opened or closed the switches on a siding. During the nine years that Jack operated the tower, he never made an error that caused a mishap.

Chips, a part collie, part husky, was one of the many heroes of World War II. Chips served with the Third Division Infantry Regiment of General George S. Patton's Seventh Army when the Allies made their landing in Sicily. They were met with a baptism of fire.

Heavy machinegun fire met Chips and his handler, Pfc.

John Roswell, when they hit the beach. Roswell decided that the fire in his immediate vicinity came from a peasant's hut that he was sure was a camouflaged gun emplacement. Before Roswell was able to inform his fellow infantrymen of his discovery, however, Chips broke loose and charged the peasant hut.

Roswell reported that there was a lot of noise and the firing stopped. First one Italian soldier emerged from the hut and then three other machinegunners surrendered. They appeared to be in a state of shock from the dog's savage attack, according to Roswell.

Captain Edward Paar's recommendation for Chips to be awarded the Distinguished Service Cross read: ''The dog's courageous action in single-handedly eliminating a dangerous machine-gun nest and causing the surrender of its crew reflects the highest credit on himself and the military service.''

Perhaps the most famous tracking dog of all time was Nick Carter, a bloodhound whose dedication to his job resulted in the conviction of more than six hundred criminals. He was owned and trained by Capt. Volney G. Mullikan. Nick and the detective were quite a pair. They relentlessly pursued their quarry over Kentucky and West Virginia mountains so rough that the dog's feet bled and over city streets where hundreds of people had passed meanwhile. Nick could pick a trail four days old or even track a man on horseback. He became so well known that several criminals gave up when they learned he had been brought in on the case.

We have come to expect highly trained police dogs to be able to patrol, stand guard, trail, pursue, attack upon command, and to hold captives. We do not anticipate that a dog can also serve as a detective. The German shepherd Dox was a highly successful investigator, could untie complicated knots, and unload a pistol without firing it.

Dox won Europe's annual policedog match crown in 1953 and successfully defended his title for years against such veteran canines as Rex of Scotland Yard and Xorro of the Paris Police. By the time he was fourteen years old he had won four gold medals and twenty-seven silver medals and possessed the scars of seven bullet wounds acquired in his native Italy.

The Gaddises quote Dr. Carmelo Marzano, commanding officer of Rome's police department, as saying: "Dox may have been born a dog, but he is no longer just a dog. He has probably cracked more cases than any other detective on the force. We consider him one of our best men."

Dox was owned and trained by Police Sergeant Giovanni Maimone and for years they were inseparable.

It seems that Dox's memory was phenomenal. One day Maimone and Dox entered a restaurant in Rome and the big German shepherd suddenly jumped a man who was eating a plate of spaghetti. It was discovered that the man was a wanted fugitive who had eluded Dox six years earlier in Turin.

The sergeant's newspaper clippings on his dog filled five large scrapbooks. The articles told how Dox had once kept twelve suspects standing with raised arms while Maimone called in for help; of the time the dog saved a small child's life by pushing her from the path of a speeding car; of when he found a lost skier in the Subiaco mountains after a posse of men and dogs had failed; and the time when he caught a burglar after a three-mile chase on three legs after one was broken by a bullet.

What made Dox famous, however, was his ability to solve a crime entirely on his own. One night he was put on the trail of a burglar who had overpowered the night watchman at a Rome jewelry store. Dox picked up the trail from the watchman's clothing and an abandoned tool. The dog led officers to a cellar apartment but the occupant managed to convince the policemen that he was innocent.

Dox wouldn't settle for this, however. He barked at Maimone and started off. The detective followed. The shepherd led Maimone back to the jewelry store and entered a rear storeroom. There he picked up a button and dropped it in Maimone's hand. Dox gave another bark, indicating he wanted his master and the other officers to follow. He led them back to the suspect's apartment. There he sniffed in a closet, pulled a raincoat from a hanger, and placed it at Maimone's feet. The coat was missing a button—like the one found in the jewelry store. The suspect confessed.

Stories have been told how people have been saved from freezing when their pets huddled next to them and kept them warm. One can easily argue, however, that the animals did this to save their own skins.

But how can we explain the following tale of wild animals—toughened to the elements and having no need for human warmth—saving the life of a lost twelve-year-old youngster?

According to the Central Press of Canada, in November 1956, Rheal Guindon, of Opatsitka, Ontario, went on a fishing trip with his parents. Rheal was not in the boat when it overturned and his parents were drowned. Frightened and grief-stricken, the youngster set out for Kapuskasing, the closest town. That night the temperature fell below zero. Lost, exhausted, and chilled to the bone, Rheal lay on the ground and prayed.

Suddenly, in the darkness, the boy felt something furry against him. He didn't know what kind of animal it was, but it was warm, so he put his arms around it and huddled close. He cried himself to sleep. It was morning when he awoke, and lying across and against him were three large beavers. He arrived in Kapuskasing late that morning, his feet bleeding, but he was alive.

A small spitz dog who served as night nurse for his diabetic mistress is mentioned by Dr. Gustav Eckstein in his book *Everyday Miracle*. The dog slept in the crook of the woman's arm. He would awaken instantly if her breathing rhythm changed, indicative of slipping into a coma. The little dog would dash into an adjoining room and awaken the woman's daughter. According to Dr. Eckstein, a dog would be quicker than a physician in detecting the advance of coma from the breathing.

Throughout *Kinship with All Life* J. Allen Boone stressed the need of the human being to recognize that real communication and rapport with animals depended largely upon respect for their intelligence and feelings. Without this acceptance, he explained, animals might be trained to obey human commands but there could be no real sharing.

One of the greatest demonstrations of this two-way communication was revealed by John Solomon Rorey, probably the world's greatest wild horse trainer. During the middle of the nineteenth century the breaking of horses, or, for that matter, the training of any animals, was based on fear. But Rorey got along with the worst of the lot with love, kindness, and an amazing ability to understand the thoughts and feelings of his students. Ralph Waldo Emerson once said of him, "John Rorey has turned a new leaf for civilization."

No one ever knew Rorey's secret, for he always insisted on being alone when he tamed a wild horse. His talent emerged when he was twelve years old. His father, Adam Rorey, had brought home to their farm near Columbus, Ohio, an incorrigible colt. It was well bred but cheap, as the former owner had given up on him after a dozen professional horse-breakers failed to tame the animal. Deciding to show the colt who was boss, Adam struck him with a whip. The horse reacted by snapping his halter rope and slamming the man against a fence with such violence that he broke his leg.

Convinced the horse was insane, Adam ordered one of his hands to shoot him. The man, along with some neighbors, started for the barn, but before they arrived young Rorey emerged from the barn astride the animal that no one had been able to get close to.

Rorey's fame spread quickly after this incident. Horses from all over the country were brought to him to break. If he kept them a few days, he would also teach them to bow, kneel, and canter. At the age of nineteen, Rorey was challenged in Texas to conquer five of the meanest horses the Texans could round up. Four of the horses had each killed a man and the fifth had crippled two men.

Thousands gathered to watch what they believed to be

the death of the legendary Rorey. He ignored the betting odds against him and entered the box stall holding the first killer while the audience gasped. As the minutes passed, the odds were higher and higher in favor of the horses. But forty minutes later Rorey rode the horse out of the stall and to the center of the corral. While the crowd roared in astonishment, he dismounted, had the killer kneel and then lie on its side. The other horses were to follow with similar performances.

Internationally famous, Rorey traveled the country demonstrating that the most dangerous horse could be tamed and lecturing on kindness to animals. He traveled throughout Europe and tamed the worst horses in France, Germany, Sweden, England, Spain, and Egypt.

In England in 1868 Rorey was challenged to tame Lord Dorchester's former racing stallion. In *Strange World*, Frank Edwards relates that the horse, Cruiser, had been considered completely insane for four years. It would have spells so violent that it would bite itself and tear a wooden stall to pieces in a few minutes. It was kept in a specially constructed brick-and-steel stall.

When the group of titled persons, sportsmen, and news reporters arrived with Rorey at Cruiser's stall the horse was attacking the door in such a frenzy that it was shaking the entire structure. Lord Dorchester suddenly realized that he might well be responsible for Rorey's death. He offered to withdraw the challenge and to pay Rorey for his trouble and trip.

Rorey told Dorchester that he needn't be concerned, that all he would need was a halter and a body belt. When the horse was momentarily dazed from striking his head against the stall, Rorey slipped inside and put the halter on the horse and stepped out again. The crazed animal then attacked the halter, which was attached to a ring in the wall, until he dropped from exhaustion. Rorey slipped in again and snapped on the body belt with two straps. It was so arranged that Rorey could buckle the horse's front legs by pulling on the straps.

Rorey sat beside the horse for three hours, petting it,

stroking its neck, and talking softly to it. Whenever Cruiser struggled, Rorey gently pulled on the straps. The following day Rorey rode Cruiser through the streets of London.

John Solomon Rorey died at the age of thirty-eight but his legend and, more important, his message lives on.

One of the most fascinating stories of the rapport between man and other creatures was Boone's relationship with a common housefly he called Freddie. Boone made friends with the fly and it would join him each morning at seven o'clock by landing on his shaving mirror. Boone would invite him to climb aboard his finger and he would gently stroke his wings. Freddie paraded up and down his finger and they would play a game of Boone tossing him in the air and catching him again on the tip of his finger.

The early-morning rendezvous continued for some time and the small housefly would also come when Boone called his name. Remembering what he had learned from the wise German shepherd Strongheart, Boone reminded himself ''(1) That inherently Freddie the fly and I as living beings were inseparable parts of an interrelated, interfunctioning and all-including Totality. (2) That neither he nor I were originating causes for anything, but instead were individual living expressions of an universal divine Cause or Mind that was ever speaking and living itself through each of us and through everything else.'' He was to discover, as he had with other creatures, that much was to be learned by ''silently talking across to him. Not as to 'a fly' with all the limiting and condemning things that we humans usually fasten on flies, but as to an intelligent fellow being . . .''

Grace Wiley has made snake history at her Zoo for Happiness near Long Beach, California, by practicing this same brand of philosophy and inner communication with the snakes that are brought to her. She has learned to share with all manner of snakes with bad reputations—enormous king cobras over twenty-five feet long, Egyptian cobras, copperheads, moccasins, adders, Australian black snakes, vipers, fer-de-lances, green mambas, tigersnakes, and all kinds of rattlesnakes. She has been observed to gentle the most vicious of reptiles in less than an hour. They learn quickly that only understanding, kindness, and love will be forthcoming.

The Proberts, Boones, Roreys, Lillys, Kimballs, Lydeckers, Mojave Dans, Mad Bears, Lois Flying Clouds—those who have truly learned to communicate with animals—tell us that real sharing comes from the heart, the intuitive levels of a universal language where there are no barriers between species and the members of the Kingdom. Animals have great psychic sensitivity, and if we wish to share with them, apparently we must move beyond the limits of the rational to the deeper dimensions of the mind.

Western science has just begun to construct a model of consciousness that allows for paranormal powers. Extrasensory perception has gained general acceptance by the public, and this acceptance has encouraged people to seek the development of these talents. As more people are able to demonstrate psi skills, the more available are test subjects and the easier it is for scientists to hypothesize on a schematic of the brain and mind.

As it has been shown that animals are in many ways superior to us in their use of psi, it might be helpful for those interested in developing their psychic abilities to work with their pets in establishing, for example, telepathic communication. Dogs, cats, birds, and other common domesticated animals are excellent senders and receivers.

Rex, my neighbor's dog, seemed always able to read his mind. Rex loved to ride in the car and he could sense those occasions when he would be allowed to do so. He would run to the car and start barking when his owners were planning to go somewhere but before making any physical gestures in that direction. Yet Rex would ignore the car on work days when he knew he would not be allowed to go along.

Our basset, Sady, rides in the pickup when we are doing chores around the farm. She always seems to know when we are going to be parked for a while, at which times she will get out. If we are going to be back shortly, she will wait.

There are many stories of dogs who will wait at the edge of the driveway for their masters to come home from work, seeming always to know how to time their ritual several minutes before the car is in sight. But if their master is to be gone overnight, they will dispense with the welcoming gesture until the date and close to the time of arrival.

The Rev. Charlie W. Shedd, D. D., pastor of the Memorial Drive Presbyterian Church in Houston, Texas, reported in the Houston *Post*, May 15, 1966, that one of his parishioners had an unusual ESP experience with one of her horses. The young woman lived in the city and her two riding horses were pastured in the country five miles away. She was awakened one morning at two o'clock by a horse neighing. Knowing there were no horses anywhere near her city environment, she tried to go back to sleep. But the neighing came again, loud and clear, and with it the premonition that she should go to the pasture.

"How silly can you get?" she was quoted as asking herself. "Are you losing your mind? It's two o'clock in the morning!"

The compulsion was too strong for her to resist, however, so she dressed, and drove to the pasture. There in the beam of her flashlight was her palomino mare standing in tangled wire neighing her lungs out. The horse stood still while her mistress untangled the fencing and freed her hooves with little more damage than minor scratches.

A woman once told the naturalist Archibald Rutledge that her setter Marcella knew when her master died. The story was told in the April 1946 issue of *Magazine Digest*.

The woman's husband was away overnight on a business trip. The dog awakened her in the middle of the night by its growling. She turned on the light and the dog was standing at the door and her hair was bristled. "Her voice was deep and hoarse and strange," the woman stated and added that Marcella acted as though she was filled with dread and seeing something that she could not see. The setter then howled mournfully and ran to a closet whimpering and cowering, which was very strange behavior for the usually brave dog.

Within half an hour the news came that Marcella's master had been killed in a car wreck. "In some way," the woman told Rutledge, "I believe Marcella saw it all."

Richard H. Lee of Prescott, Arizona, was killed in an automobile accident one night in Phoenix. His wife learned of his death around midnight. The following morning she noticed that her husband's beloved black tomcat was highly excited. He would not enter the house, nor would he allow Mrs. Lee to touch him.

She wrote in the *Arizona Republic*: "When I took some food out to him he climbed the stone wall back of the house in a perfect panic." The cat remained in the neighborhood. Occasionally Mrs. Lee would see him watching the home, but if she tried to draw close he ran away.

The story of Flak, the canine mascot of a bomber crew during World War II, was told by John and June Robbins in an article in *This Week* magazine in 1960. Flak remained aloof from other airmen at the base in Tunis, North Africa, but he always appeared on the field just before his six masters' plane returned from its mission.

One day while his crew was on a mission, Flak began howling very loudly and sorrowfully. He would not be comforted, and when the planes returned from their missions, Flak, for the first time, refused to go out on the flight line to meet them. Somehow he knew that the plane bearing his crew had been shot down over Italy shortly before noon.

Duke was a registered pointer who displayed highly developed extrasensory powers. His story was told in *Exploring the Unknown*, Vol. 3, No. 3, and again by the Gaddises in the book mentioned earlier.

It seems that Duke was given to K. G. Dee when he was a boy. While Dee was at school, Duke, in order to remain busy, made the rounds with a deliveryman named Fred. Whenever Fred stopped to deliver a package, Duke remained on the seat of the wagon and held the horse's rein in his mouth. But when it came time for school to be out, Duke hightailed it home to be with Dee.

One day Fred told the senior Dee that Duke was so smart that it gave him the creeps. He explained that the dog understood every word that he spoke to him. Whenever he took a day off he would tell Duke that deliveries would not be made the following day and that he was not to come to the store. Duke never showed up on those days. When Fred was going on vacation, he told Duke not to show up until a week later, and, sure enough, Duke was never seen around the store or delivery wagon until it was time for Fred to return.

At one time Mr. Dee decided to run against the local butcher for a city office. During this period the young Dee had a paper route and the butcher was one of his customers. Until the campaign, Duke had accompanied the boy into the shop for handouts. But from then on he refused to enter the meat market. Instead he stood outside and growled while Dee went inside. The butcher won the election and Duke never again entered the store.

An explanation of why most people do not receive telepathic messages was offered by British parapsychologist H. H. Price, a professor of logic at Oxford University. He told the Society for Psychical Research in London: ". . . the reason most of us appear to receive no telepathic impressions is that we may receive too many, so that no one of them makes any distinct or individual mark upon our minds."

It may be that we keep our brains so busy computing data from our five senses that we pay little attention to the worlds of information reaching our supersenses. Animals, less belabored by the complexities of life, are more in tune with nature and the psychic dimensions than ourselves.

Naturalist John Burroughs called it the hidden heart of nature, and some Indians refer to it as deep-knowing. Carl G. Jung described an intelligence beyond individual intellect, the great collective unconscious, the depository of all memories, thoughts, and knowledge, spaceless and timeless. This mental reservoir is the same everywhere and all forms of life partake of and are enveloped within it. Living together within this Universal Being, individual minds, regardless of the physical form they seem to inhabit, become aware of each other in a new medium and share in ways never experienced before.

12

Animal Language

"For all these living entities, like man, possess not only an outer physical form but an inner spiritual component. Indians must kill a deer or fell a pine in order to utilize its physical form for their material needs. But before doing so, they invoke its spiritual life as a source of psychic energy also. Such rituals were conducted throughout all America and Ancient Mexico, and they are still observed today in the Southwest. As I see it, we must graduate to this belief, to attune ourselves to both the inner and outer realities of life if we are to close the widening rupture between our minds and hearts. By rupture, I mean this. In ruthlessly destroying nature, man, who is also part of nature, ruptures his own inner self. For man's unconscious is equated to and rooted in nature. And by our destructive and materialistic rationalism, we have alienated our conscious self from the earthy substratum of our essential being . . . We've got to listen to the voice of the secret and invisible spirit of the land itself."

When I discovered this passage, I read it several times. It made me remember the words of Lois Flying Cloud spoken to me many years ago: "If you will learn to listen to the wind when it calls," she said, "and discover the language of other animals than ourselves, you will never lose the center of yourself.''

The passage quoted above was from an interview that James Peterson conducted with Frank Waters. It was published in the May 1973 issue of *Psychology Today* and was entitled ''Lessons from the Indian Soul.'' Frank Waters, author of *The Colorado Book of the Hopi* and *The Man Who Killed the Deer*, is considered today's foremost writer on the American Indian. What is so appealing about Waters' writing is that one is told that language can be a great deal more than a rosary of words, that the deepest, most profound communication comes from the heart and not the mind.

What was so hauntingly beautiful about *Jonathan Livingston Seagull* was not that the book was a modern mythology presenting hidden truths in an allegorical fashion. Certainly, it was this, but while one understood that the story pertained to man's sojourn upon this and other worlds, the reader was almost equally sure that the story was also about seagulls. He would tell himself that it was not, committed as we are to the Judeo-Christian belief that immortality is reserved for our own species. But something within our unconscious domains, or at the intuitive levels of our hearts, tells us we share our destiny with the great white bird. The delight and optimism we experienced in reading the words, which Bach himself claimed came to him from another dimension, defied any logical convictions to the contrary, and we found ourselves basking at least for the moment in a certain knowledge that all of life is one.

Job tells us, ''But ask now the beasts, and they shall teach thee; and the fowls of the air, and they shall tell thee . . .'' We have a tendency to equate communication with words; even assigning descriptive phrases to music and art, forgetting that they are a language in themselves. If one is to comment accurately on music, he must do so with music, and to a painting he must respond with a painting. Words have made us forget our beginnings. We have used them to chronicle our experiences through the ages. They have been the building blocks of civilizations. But they have taken us away from ourselves, and we have imagined that to label something is to understand it. Words have been our passport out of Eden, but they have served to alienate us from the other inhabitants of this planet. Perhaps we imagined they had nothing to offer us . . . except their flesh, their labor, their loyalty and devotion. Apparently we were wrong. We may even discover we are not the wisest dwellers in the kingdom. In any case, we are beginning to listen to other voices in the wind.

In the course of this chapter we will explore the efforts of some animals to master our language, perhaps despairing of our ever respecting theirs; we will take a look at communication between animals and between animals and man; more important, we will share the experiences of those individuals who have moved beyond the limitation of form to share mystically with other creatures and, thereby, touch the rim of Consciousness itself.

Not since our early childhood have we been amazed that parrots and parakeets can speak human language. A few years later we learned that crows, magpies, and jackdaws could accomplish the same feat with a little coaxing. Austrian ethnologist and animal psychologist Konrad Lorenz is of the opinion that some parrots at least are not just mimicking the human voice but "these sounds may occasionally have a definite thought association."

In *King Solomon's Ring*, Lorenz notes that many gray parrots will say "Good morning" only at the appropriate time during the day and only once to an individual. Lorenz' friend Professor Otto Koehler owned an ancient gray parrot that answered to the name of Geier, meaning "vulture" in German. Lorenz stated that Geier had unusual speaking talents and would say "Na, auf Wiedersehen," but only if the guest really departed.

Koehler and Lorenz endeavored to trick the parrot by having someone pretend to leave, even to going out the door, but Geier remained silent. On the other hand, if a person tried to slip inconspicuously out the door but was actually leaving, the bird would holler, "Na, auf Wiedersehen!"

M. Hachet-Souplet, director of the Institut de Psychologie Zoologique in Paris, taught a parrot to say the word "cupboard" when shown a little box in which his food was stored. The box was hung on the wall and Hachet-Souplet would climb a small ladder to reach the box. Each time he climbed the ladder, the bird was trained to say "climb." One day Hachet-Souplet hung the box high on the wall of his laboratory and the ladder was tucked away in a corner of the room. The parrot was presented with the problem of solving how his benefactor could reach the box filled with hempseed. Until he solved the problem, the bird was to be fed millet, for which he had little taste.

On the first day the parrot screamed, "Cupboard! Cupboard! Cupboard!" and bit at the bars of his cage, angry that he had to eat millet. On the second day, after quite a fuss, his attention became focused on the ladder. After a moment he said, "Ladder, climb, cupboard!" He got his hempseed.

Susy Smith, author of a number of exciting books on psychic phenomena and paranormal talents, told me an interesting story recently over a cup of coffee in her home in Tucson. An inhabitant of Parrot Jungle in Miami, a macaw, made a statement one day that was quite appropriate but one he had not been taught nor had ever uttered.

Mrs. Franz Scherr, wife of the owner, took care of the tickets at the entrance gate and one day got in an argument with a man over the price of admission. She assured the man that no exception could be made and he turned to leave in a huff. The macaw was lounging on a perch nearby at the time and as the man retreated, mumbling profanities, the bird called out, "Go to hell!" It had been pronounced in a voice so like that of Mrs. Scherr that the irate tourist turned and gave her a venomous look. The bird "was a gentleman coming to the defense of a lady in the best way he knew how," Susy said.

Experiments with chimpanzees have revealed that they have at least thirty-two distinct sounds. All of these have been mechanically recorded. The sounds have been found to express the emotions of anxiety, fear, hunger, anger, etc., as well as small talk between members of the group.

Judy, the chimpanzee who acted in TV's *Daktari* series, knew 125 verbal commands. Anthropoid vocabularies have been reported by Dr. R. L. Garner and the German scientist, Georg Schwidetsky. In *Animal I.Q.*, Vance Packard quotes Schwidetsky as having expressed the belief that certain anthropoid words are identical to root words found in ancient China and also used by the Bushmen of South Africa.

Attempts to teach apes our language have never succeeded beyond getting them to repeat a few words. However, in recent years studies have been made of the chimpanzee's spontaneous gestures and it was found that chimpanzees and children use sign languages that are similar in several respects. Dr. W. M. Kellogg attempted to teach a chimpanzee the sign language used by the deaf and dumb and found this chimpanzee learned to understand and use nineteen signs in little more than a year. Some of these signs were verbs and adjectives that the chimpanzee used correctly in varying contexts.

Some success has been realized in teaching elephants to distinguish between visual symbols, and they have learned to write a little on a machine with easily legible letters. Karl-Erik Fichtelius and Sverre Sjolander explain, however, in their book *Smarter Than Man?*, that elephants have very poor vision, while the sensitivity at the tip of their trunks is quite fantastic. This being the case, the authors stress that we should work with an animal according to his strengths, not his weaknesses, and they ask why we do not use braille with elephants.

It has been estimated that the average pet has an understanding of approximately sixty words, but some animals are believed to understand several hundred words. A German shepherd by the name of Fellow was tested at Columbia and New York University and was found to understand more than three hundred words. According to George and Helen Papashvily, authors of *Dogs and People*, it was the actual words and not the tone of the voice or clues that Fellow grasped. When familiar commands were rearranged into other phrases, the dog still understood. His owner stated that he never said anything to the German shepherd without a purpose and never rewarded or punished him except by saying, "Good dog," or "What a shame."

A talking dog made quite a hit in the 1940s. Blitz was a large shepherd who lived in the Bronx. Paul Phelan of the New York *Sun* "interviewed" Blitz at Public School 48, where his master, Arthur J. Devlin, was custodian. Phelan said he was speechless when the dog muttered, "Good morning, I want my mommie."

Devlin stated that he discovered his dog's speaking ability in 1942 when he said to Blitz, as he had many times before, "Do you want to go out?" and the dog aarfed, "Want out." Disbelieving what he had heard, Devlin called in a neighbor and the dog repeated his performance.

Devlin told Phelan that he could never be sure what the dog would say. He recounted an incident when he had taken Blitz into a tavern in Bay Ridge. "I gave him a quarter and he put his paws upon the bar, laid the quarter down, and said, 'I want a hamburger.' The bartender dropped a glass of beer and went into shock."

A Boston terrier named Mr. Lucky had a vocabulary of a number of words. He was tested by Dr. William Perkins of the University of Southern California's Speech Clinic. Dr. Perkins recorded Mr. Lucky's speaking voice and found it to be thin and high, much like that of a talking doll. His natural bark, however, was deep. While the dog had some difficulty in pronouncing some consonants, his speech was understandable.

Salt Lake City *News* reporter Jack E. Jarrard interviewed the terrier and wrote, "He doesn't talk just unintelligible gruntings that can be interpreted as words, but makes recognizable words and sentences."

Mr. Lucky's owner, Mrs. J. T. Davis, of Midvale, Utah, told reporters that she stayed too long at a next-door neighbor's house one day and the dog, who was with her and evidently was getting bored, declared, "Aw, come on home."

One cannot help but wonder what role imagination plays in these conversational encounters. However, when talking abilities of these animals are confirmed by several persons, disinterested individuals among them, one cannot discount the reports. Missie, for example, performed for dozens of people. Another dog, Pepe, a Chihuahua, made a reputation for himself as a talking dog several years ago.

Allegedly, Pepe stuck his head in the air and burst forth with singsong syllables such as "I love you" and other little endearments. Clare Adele Lambert described the procedure in the July 1966 issue of *Fate* magazine: "A little singing sound starts in Pepe's throat as his muscles begin to move. Then he lifts his head high, opens his mouth wide and sings the words in a loud voice for so small an animal." She claimed that Pepe did not speak in a monotone. "He sings rather than talks, although really it is a combination of both. With each phrase he goes up and down the scale using three or more tones."

Pepe was owned by Jerry Genovas of Torrance, California. He appeared on television a number of times. Author Susy Smith, on the other hand, was not convinced of Pepe's speaking abilities. Although she did not actually hear Pepe himself, she queried a number of people who had heard Pepe in person or on television. The consensus was divided, Susy told me. Several were of the opinion that the dog spoke words, comparing the sound with a child learning to talk. Others, however, felt that it was more Pepe's intonation which made it seem as if he were talking.

Studies have shown that chickens have a vocabulary of about twenty-five signals. Deer rattle their antlers against trees or shrubs to send word along to others. They have also been known to paw the ground when danger is imminent. An elk will give a short snort as a danger signal and the herd will take instant flight. When one of the leaders of the herd makes a particular motion of the head, the entire herd will turn in the direction indicated.

Konrad Lorenz discovered that when a wolf is losing a fight to another, he puts his tail between his legs and bares his throat. This is believed to be an invitation to his opponent to kill him. Yet, apparently this seldom or never happens. The defeated wolf is allowed to sneak away.

Crested larks have the ability to imitate human voices, but zoologists have recorded one crested lark in particular that could sing seven human songs and repeat other words and numbers, according to Vitus B. Droscher. In *The Friendly Beast* Droscher relates that two Erlanger larks used their skills to confuse a shepherd and his dogs. The shepherd used whistles to give commands to his dogs, and they had been carefully codified. A rising scale of five whistles, the last being much lower in pitch, meant "run away!" One or more sharp whistles signified varying degrees of "hurry!" A quivering long-drawn-out whistle meant for the dogs to stop whatever they were doing and to come to him immediately.

The larks mastered all of these signals, and the dogs became quite frustrated between the sounds produced by their master and his imitators. The dogs could not distinguish the difference and learned not to act until the signal was confirmed by a hand gesture.

Dr. Erwin Iretzel, an ornithologist, made a sonicspectrographic comparison of the shepherd's whistles with those of the larks. It turned out that the shepherd was not very musical, seldom hitting the same pitch twice. Nor did he have an accurate sense of timing. The little larks, however, suffered from no such inadequacies. They reproduced the sounds they had learned with consistent exactitude, using the whole-tone intervals of the C-major scale with never a flat note.

"These findings led to a further question: If there are always such flaws in tune and rhythm in their model, how do the larks establish a standard for their own performance?" Droscher asks. "It may seem fantastic to say, but the birds clearly act on their own initiative. They transpose what they had heard in a manner that suits their own dispositions."

In Dr. Iretzel's words: "The lark had grasped the 'idea,' the ideal form of this motif, and whistled it as the shepherd probably thought he was rendering it but seldom actually succeeded in doing . . . The lark produced all the shepherd's whistles far more purely and musically, more delicately in tone and more elegantly in scale. In musical terms, it refined the whistles, as it were. Here an astonishing feeling for form and metrics has been displayed by a bird that no one has hitherto thought a good singer. Certainly no one would have suspected that there were principles of order underlying the jabbering medleys it produces."

The case of the larks is not an isolated one and they cannot be cited as feathered prodigies. In 1966 Dr. Iretzel was quoted by the German press as having observed the same phenomenon in ordinary blackbirds in the garden of Garmisch-Partenkirchen. The blackbirds imitated the whistles that a man used to call his cat. This was a hazardous course for the blackbirds, for the cat was seen leaping at one of the birds foolish enough to call him. The same destructive gesture was made by a parrot owned by my wife's family when she was a child. The parrot would sometimes get out of his cage and perch in a nearby tree. Immediately he would start hollering, "Here, kitty, kitty," while the family in a panic tried to get him back in the house.

Johannes Kneutgen at the Max Planck Institute in Seewiesen conducted an experiment with a magpie robin. While the bird was singing, Kneutgen placed a metronome near it. The robin responded to the ticking instrument much like an opera singer to her conductor, fitting the tempo of the song exactly to the beat of the metronome. When the tempo was slowly increased, the bird endeavored to keep pace. But as the instrument continued to increase the tempo, the bird finally decided the pace should not be speeded up any further. Instead, the robin switched to another tune in its repertory, one "whose natural tempo corresponded to the speed of the obtrusive instrument.

Could there be any better evidence that birds have a feeling for the beauty of musical forms?'' Droscher asks.

Droscher explains that many scientists agree that the songs of birds present more than an expression of utilitarian ends. More than just war chants and staking out territorial rights, or love songs, the singing has an aesthetic quality surpassing basic communication. Droscher asks, ''. . . are these birds producing something that can be regarded as a preliminary step toward art?'' He answers, ''After decades of investigation many scientists believe that such an assumption is justified.''

Lorenz commented on this: ''We know that birdsong reaches its highest perfection and its highest virtuosity where it does not serve the functions of delimiting territory, luring the female and intimidating a rival. A blue-throat, a doyal, a blackbird, sing their most artful songs only when they are singing creatively to themselves, in an altogether temperate mood. When the song is aimed at some purpose, when the bird is singing at an opponent or making a display for a female, all the higher subtleties are lost.''

Dr. Eberhard Gwinner studied several ravens at the Max Planck Institute for Behavioral Physiology in Bavaria. Ravens are thought to be quite intelligent, for they not only caw, and produce various sounds picked up from their environment, but they can imitate the human voice better than a parrot. One of Dr. Gwinner's ravens, named Wotan, enjoyed imitating the barking of dogs, while another of his ravens, Freya, Wotan's mate, liked to gobble like a turkey.

One day Wotan disappeared and Freya, desperate to find him, did something she had never done before. She started using her mate's favorite sound, barking. And Wotan, in turn, responded with Freya's turkey gobble, a sound he had not practiced before. Continuing their calls, the birds found one another. They immediately returned to their own favorite sounds. Kneutgen, at the same institution, meanwhile discovered that doyals will use their mate's favorite call whenever the straying member has been away too long. This business of "calling by name" does not seem to be limited to a particular species.

Droscher in the above-mentioned book reported that Kneutgen observed young doyals attending school. Five babies flew out of the nest to a nearby tree and perched on either side of their father. He then proceeded to instruct them. First he sang a tune to them while they listened attentively with cocked heads. After a time they began to sing along with their father very softly and still listening. The father continued to repeat a melody until all of the children struck every note correctly.

American entomologist Edward O. Wilson discovered that ants combine several odors to make mixtures. By this method the ants develop more "words" in their vocabulary than the mere number of scent glands in their bodies. Professor Wilson stated in "Pheromones," which appeared in a 1963 issue of *Scientific American*, that it appeared that the insects can emit their signal odors at different rates of speed and modulate each emission so that odors of varying strength result. The ants thus create a kind of Morse code.

It is when we move into the utterly amazing world of the dolphin, however, that we have to question our claim to superiority. A hundred stories and almost as many studies tell of the extraordinary intelligence, tolerance, patience, and selfless love of these creatures.

I met my first dolphins fishing off the Florida coast for mackerel and was not kindly disposed toward them. They playfully danced and bounded behind our boat and discouraged any mackerel within a half-mile of us. But I soon learned to enjoy their early-morning demonstrations, for off the shore a short distance from our cottage they would group and play follow-the-leader. Whatever the lead dolphin would do, the others would imitate in perfect timing and unison.

They protected our shores from sharks. While I had heard many stories of dolphins protecting or saving humans in the water, I gave these tales little thought. But one day while skindiving for lace coral on a nearby reef I was suddenly shocked to see a large torpedo-shaped figure moving toward me in the water. I immediately thought "shark!" and frantically lunged toward the surface. The next instant it was right next to me and I was overjoyed to discern that it was a dolphin. He hung close as I swam, but when I broke the surface and he was assured that I could comfortably reach my boat he departed as quickly as he had arrived.

An elderly neighbor of ours relied on the dolphins for his means of returning home after a sea voyage. Several times a week this man would lie on his back in a large inflated truck tire tube and allow the wake of the surf to carry him seaward. While he could have been washed a dangerous distance away from the shore, this never occured. Some watchful dolphin would decide that he had gone far enough and promptly push him back to the shore.

Vincent and Margaret Gaddis propose that barring possible contact with intelligences from outer space, our first complex conversations with nonhumans will likely be with dolphins.

Scientists are still breathless over the discovery that dolphins have larger cerebral cortexes than ourselves, and this gray folded blanket enveloping the rest of our brain and supposedly providing us with superior reasoning power is more complex in the dolphin than in ourselves.

Several years ago the U.S. Navy sought a special study of the large sea mammals at its Communications Research Institute in the Virgin Islands. The Navy hoped to learn from the dolphin's efficient swimming skills how to design an improved submarine. The study was placed under the direction of Dr. John C. Lilly, a neurophysiologist. No one dreamed, including Lilly, how important the discoveries would be.

Dr. Lilly had to use a computer to keep pace with the dolphins. He found that their brains work incredibly fast compared to humans'. Colin Taylor, curator of the Port Elizabeth Oceanarium in South Africa, has estimated that dolphins' brains work sixteen times faster than a man's. He questions, however, if they retain as much information.

Dr. Lilly placed an electrode in the "pleasure center" of a dolphin's brain. He said the dolphin learned in one try to turn on the switch producing the current. Monkeys generally have to make several hundred tries to learn this technique.

In his book *Man and Dolphin*, Dr. Lilly tells how a young dolphin wandered out of sight of his group and was attacked by three sharks. He started uttering a series of distress signals, short twin whistles, the first rising sharply in pitch and the second half falling just as abruptly in pitch.

The effect was quite amazing. More than twenty dolphins, who were carrying on a lively discussion at the time, immediately stopped their conversation. Absolute silence prevailed. Then the dolphins raced toward the scene of the attack at their top speed, approximately forty miles per hour. The male dolphins rammed the sharks without slowing their speed and soon the cartilaginous skeletons of the sharks were shattered and they sank lifeless to the bottom of the sea.

Meanwhile, the females went to the assistance of the badly injured young dolphin. He could not surface by his own strength. Two of the females placed themselves on either side of him, put their flippers under him, and raised him to the surface so that his blowhole was above the water and he could breathe. This maneuver was carefully carried out by an exchange of whistling signals. From time to time the females relieved one another. Dolphins have been known to give this kind of aid to an injured member for two weeks, day and night, until a full recovery was made.

German psychiatrist G. Pilleri is quoted by Droscher as saying that the dolphin's brain "attains a degree of centralization far beyond that of man . . . the ultimate status of man's brain in the ranking of mammals is today beginning to be a matter of doubt." And physicist and biologist Leo Szilard predicted in *The Voice of the Dolphin and Other Stories* that if man should ever learn to talk to dolphins those "intellectuals of the sea would win all the

Nobel Prizes for physics, chemistry and medicine, and the Peace Prize to boot.''

Rather convincing proof that dolphins carry on actual dialogue was provided when Dr. Lilly divided two dolphins in a pool by a panel of sheet metal. First the dolphins produced a shrill concert of whistles. They could recognize each other's sounds even though they could not see each other. They tried to leap high enough to see each other but failed.

They both fell into silence. After a time, however, the male started encouraging his mate to converse with him. He carried on quite an extensive monologue before she responded. When she did finally speak, the male became silent until she had finished. This alternation of sound production continued for varying periods of time.

The dolphin has been found to be sensitive to sounds up to 150,000 cycles per second and to emit sounds up to 120,000 cps. They produce two primary sounds, whistling noises and a series of rapidly repeated clicks, with frequencies up to the 120,000 cps level. The clicks are used in echo location and are emitted most of the time.

Laboratory tests have shown that the sonar system of dolphins is better than that of the bat. In order to test this, rubber cups were fitted over the dolphins' eyes so that they could not see. Despite being temporarily blinded the dolphins swam around their tanks at high speeds without bumping into obstacles. They could catch fish thrown into the water, and one dolphin, according to Maurice Burton in his *The Sixth Sense of Animals*, was able to distinguish between a gelatin capsule filled with water and a fish of the same size.

It is believed that the evolution of language goes hand in hand with the development of the cerebrum. In *Smarter Than Man?* Karl-Erik Fichtelius and Sverre Sjolander state that there is much to indicate that in mammals ''there is a critical absolute brain size below which language is impossible and above which language is not only possible but even probable. Modern information theory holds that the number of interconnecting active elements determines functional capacity . . . The normal speaking and writing human brain contains 13 billion interconnecting neurons and 65 billion glia . . . And in regard to the number of elements, the dolphin brain is superior to the human.''

Fichtelius and Sjolander state that another requirement for language is that there must be something to communicate and that neuroanatomical research has shown ''that the dolphin can take in as much information by means of its vision and hearing as we can. Like us, they are social animals and ought to have as much to communicate as prehistoric man, who very definitely had a language.

''A third prerequisite is of course some means of expression. The dolphin is certainly not deficient here.''

Dr. Lilly found that dolphins employ frequencies four and a half times higher than those used by humans and that they can manage four and a half times as much information per unit of time as man. As the dolphin has two separate sets of sound-producing apparatus, one in each half of its blowhole, and they can be used simultaneously, Dr. Lilly believes that the dolphin should be able to emit nine times as much information as the human can per unit of time.

Dr. Kenneth S. Norris at the Makapuu Oceanographic Institute in Hawaii had his Pacific dolphins carry on a dialogue via telephone with Atlantic members of the species in the marine laboratories in Miami. An underwater microphone, telephone cables, and an underwater loudspeaker were rigged for the occasion. Some amazing results were produced. Each dolphin let the other finish speaking before replying.

Encouraged by the telephone project, two naval engineers, T. G. Lang and H. A. P. Smith of the U.S. Naval Ordnance Test Station in Pasadena, California, were inspired to further test the speaking proficiencies of dolphins. A couple, Doris and Dash, were placed in two separate soundproof tanks and were provided with an underwater telephone. The experimenters were able to interrupt the telephone connection whenever they liked.

Doris and Dash were instantly aware when the connection was and was not functioning. Through their alternating exchange of sound, the dolphins expressed themselves very tersely. Neither talked for more than five seconds at a time. If no reply was forthcoming, he or she dropped into silence. At certain intervals the dolphins uttered a few sounds, perhaps to check whether the other was again on the phone.

Drs. John Dreher, William E. Evans, and J. H. Prescott of the Lockheed Aircraft Corporation listened in on five bottlenose dolphins with sensitive electronic listening devices. They placed fifteen buoys across the mouth of Scammon Lagoon, about three hundred miles south of San Diego, California. The dolphins made their home in the lagoon and the buoys were placed in their absence. When they returned from an extended expedition in the ocean, they sighted the buoys. They abruptly stopped, turned away, and huddled at a safe distance.

They talked back and forth for a minute and then one of the dolphins acting as a scout detached himself from the group and cautiously approached the buoys, moving from one to the next. He returned to his companions and the group exchanged a shrill burst of whistles. Following this discussion, a second dolphin left to inspect the buoys. When he returned, there was a second vehement exchange of whistling. Once reassured, all of the dolphins moved forward silently and cautiously past the buoys and into the lagoon.

The Associated Press reported from Moscow on October 18, 1967, that a school of dolphins in the Black Sea requested help from a fishing vessel. The small boat was suddenly surrounded by a number of dolphins and they proceeded to push the boat in the direction of a buoy. The Russian fishermen found a young dolphin caught in the anchor rope of the buoy. The men were able to free the dolphin baby and when they succeeded the dolphin troop let out with whistles of joy. They escorted the fishing boat all the way back to port.

The accidental discovery that dolphins mimic human

voices presented the exciting possibility of eventual communication between man and the dolphin.

One day a dolphin imitated the sounds of Dr. Lilly's laboratory equipment. He played a tape of the sounds at one quarter its normal speed. His own voice gave the tape footage, "three—two—eight," and the dolphin instantly and clearly repeated the words in a high-pitched whistle. The discovery was confirmed when other tapes of what seemed to be squawks, clicks, and whistles were played at the slower speed and the imitation of the human voice emerged. It was found that the dolphins were repeating the sounds in the laboratory, including laughter, but were doing so at a rate eight times faster than human speech.

Writing in the September 1966 issue of the *National Geographic*, Robert Conly stated that he heard a dolphin speak distinct English. "At the start of a practice session I've heard him say cheerfully to his trainer, 'All right, let's go!' He could also count from one to ten."

In the May 1965 *Newsletter* of the Communications Research Institute Dr. Lilly stated: "One cannot work with an enthusiastic dolphin for a half-hour of continuous high-speed vocal exchange day after day for months at a time without being convinced that the dolphin is trying to communicate. Not only is he trying but he is doing a better job of it than the human investigators. Dolphins can mimic and even use several physical features of human speech so well that it is uncanny to hear it."

Dr. Lilly conducted some experiments with a series of syllables. He spoke a number of these sounds in a certain order to a dolphin named Elver. In eighty-two to ninety-two percent of instances, Elver gave back the correct sound and in the right order for a series of ten, something extremely difficult for a human to duplicate.

Science writer Arthur C. Clarke has suggested that since dolphins have no written records, they could have an oral history passed down from generation to generation. The mother dolphin nurses her baby for eighteen to twenty-one months, and they remain extremely close during this period. In view of this, Dr. Lilly speculates on whether the mother teaches her baby the sum total of conception of dolphin knowledge and legends.

Perhaps we have underestimated the intelligence of animals because we have imagined that our concepts of achievement are the only ones, that the development of technology and the establishment of a complex civilization are the only indicators of growth. We have envisioned that the only intelligence is our kind: God has an infinite amount of it and animals have a small amount, but it is a matter of degree, not of kind. Since we assumed that the so-called lower creatures had nothing to teach us, we have not listened. Because of our own myopia and inadequacies, we have lived in the world, but a great deal of it has passed us by.

The secret of listening is discussed by J. Allen Boone in *Kinship with All Life*. He mentions that some people endeavor to establish communications with animals but fail to build their bridges for two-way traffic. "Their bridges permitted thought traffic to flow from them to their dogs, but not from their dogs to them. They were eager senders but not eager receivers. And that automatically threw any real correspondence out of balance."

Boone speaks of his experiences in learning to truly communicate with the great German shepherd Strongheart: "In trying to hear and understand Strongheart when he silently spoke to me, or rather when he was spoken through by the Mind of the Universe, my conventional ears were great handicaps. They were geared to harsh and discordant earth sounds and were unable to pick up the delicate universal mental language, especially as it came through a dog. I made real progress only when I gave the most diligent heed to the 'practically lost art of listening,' which, as William Butler Yeats maintained, 'is the nearest of all arts to Eternity.' "

One early evening on a hike through a meadow with Baron, my German shepherd, he suddenly stopped and sat down in front of me. I tried to move past him but he placed himself in front of me again and I realized he was trying to tell me something. He kept looking at me until

I, too, sat down in the grass, and then he turned away from me and gazed at the setting sun. His eyes fixed to the west, he sat immobile until a while after the sun had set. When he came out of his reverie, he nudged me and we took off again across the meadow, he playfully, myself in thought, in awe.

13

The Implications

In recent years there has been a tremendous breakthrough in the expansion of the human potential. The exploration of inner space has become a more exciting adventure than that of outer space, and we now know that man has possibilities we never dreamed of even a few years back. At the same time, of course, the outer-space trip has opened new doors to the universe and we stand on the threshold of new dimensions of space and time.

The particle theory of mass has crumbled, and a unified field theory which tells us that everything is related to everything else has replaced it. There is no real isolation or separation according to this model. Yet, the investigators of energy now claim that more perceptive analysis of energy provides a growing body of evidence that energy itself gives way to consciousness—the world has become a thought.

If this latest picture of the basic, underlying matrix of the universe is correct, explanations of paranormal talents, psychic phenomena, mystical experiences, and so on have a much easier time of it than when we tried to determine how mind could influence matter or vice versa. If everything resides within some level of consciousness, this problem no longer exists. Happiness is a thought and so is a table in the final analysis, and the difference resides with the observer.

The use of Kirlian photography (high-frequency photography, using an electrical field instead of light, takes pictures of the aura around parts of the body, leaves, flowers, etc.) and extremely sensitive voltmeters have provided us the means to detect the transfer of energy from a person to another individual such as in healing, or to a plant such as the successful demonstrations that sending love to experimental plants would make them grow faster than nonloved controlled plants.

That thought can be expressed as energy was demonstrated when psychics were able to radically affect the growth of plants from hundreds of miles away. Polygraph expert Cleve Backster recorded on polygraph and electroencephalograph machines the response of plants to emotional and mental input by experimenters. Marcel Vogel, senior chemist at IBM in San Jose, California, using a powerful electron microscope, measured changes of thought patterns on microscopic life forms.

A tremendous amount of research in all of these related fields has occurred during this decade, and our universe is not the same one at all that we knew as children. The old one has faded and a much greater one has taken its place. Our expanding universe has been both an external and an internal occurrence, but now we are not sure where one ends and the other one begins.

Looking through these recently discovered windows, we have begun to realize that all life is one, the expression of some all-pervading Intelligence. Nothing short of this would allow for the love that would keep Bobbie going three thousand lonely miles in search of her master, the devotion that would keep Felix at his master's grave, that would prompt Chips to risk his neck to save his company from a machinegun nest.

The evidence would seem to point to a Universal Mind in which all life has its being. Would this explain Missie's ability to foresee the future, how a swallow could return year after year to the same barn, how Duke could understand human language and make his own political decisions, how a cat could know when the weekly auction was to be held, how Rags understood that unless he kept vigil a despondent prisoner would take his own life, how dogs could return from the dead to warn their former masters of danger, how Zip knew it was Saturday and time to head for town, how Gyp could know that it was Christmas Eve and the date for his annual visit?

J. Allen Boone offers us some help on this issue. In *Kinship with All Life* he states: "... Strongheart and I were mental beings before we could possibly be objectified as material expressions of life. Therefore it was as mental beings that the dog and I had rightly to relate ourselves in order to have the rest of us rightly related, too. Whenever I worked it from this angle, Strongheart and I always moved in perfect accord . . ."

We may make a mistake in comparing animal intelligence to our own when, as separate expressions of universal consciousness, they may think as well but differently. But it is also obvious that they share many of our qualities.

It would be a mistake to assume that all animals are pure and saintly. Many cases have been cited where animals have saved human life. We should not overlook, however, those instances when pets have turned on their masters for reasons not at all clear. A relative of mine was nearly killed by a bull he had raised from a calf and treated like a pet. Only the intervention of his bulldog saved his life. Dogs, too, have been known to kill or seriously cripple those who have cared for them.

Vitus Droscher in *The Friendly Beast* describes another human failing—deceit—shared by animals, in this instance a baby beaver. He belonged to a colony that was fed every morning. Always wanting the best dainties, he was always first at the feeding place.

"One day, however," Droscher explains, "it was late for feeding time, and when it lumbered out of the water all the larger and adult beavers were already gathered around the trough. Thereupon the baby dived back into the river and slapped the water three times with its broad tail. In beaver language that is the alarm signal for extreme danger. Like a flash, all the other beavers vanished from sight in the water, and the cheeky little fellow had the feed trough to itself.''

Pets will sometimes steal food from our tables. If we argue that they do not know any better, do we use the same argument when they save our lives? Vincent and Margaret Gaddis tell the story in *The Strange World of Animals and Pets* of a cat that repented of a bad deed and tried to make amends.

It seems that Timothy was so trusted that the pet canary was allowed free flight of the house. But one day Timothy proceeded to eat the bird. He was punished for his crime and driven from the house in disgrace. But several hours later, he returned. "In his mouth he carried, unharmed, a nestling sparrow which he deposited at the feet of his mistress.''

Our usual definitions of instinct clearly do not accurately describe the quality of love and devotion demonstrated so often by animals. If survival is so important to them, why do they risk death to save the lives of humans and other animals? Curly, our half-coyote, half-shepherd, clearly understood that Skitter, our small terrier, faced being hit by a tractor. He raced in front of the machine and rolled her out of the way.

Dolphins will go to any length to save their kind and are fearless in the face of danger. "When one of the largest and most dangerous predators in the world, a thirty-footlong killer whale, dashes in among a school of dolphins, who break into shrill whistles of alarm, it might be thought that the beasts would all flee in panic—as men often do in a similar situation," Droscher states. "But that is not what occurs. First the dolphins try to rescue injured companions; only then do they make off.''

Among the many enigmas of dolphins is their kindly treatment toward us regardless of how we treat them. Droscher comments that "men have all too consistently persecuted, captured, shot, and killed dolphins. Nevertheless, not a single case has ever been recorded of a dolphin's making a hostile gesture toward a man—not even when the man is engaged in killing the dolphin.''

The Gaddises in their excellent writings on animals mention several instances where dogs have faced death to save another animal. One of their stories concerns a man named Eldon Bisbee who lived in New York City and owned a small French poodle. One night a taxicab driver came to his door with his injured dog. He told Bisbee that he had been driving through a snowstorm when he stopped to keep from hitting a German shepherd. The dog refused to get out of the way. When he shouted at the animal, it came to his window and whined and then ran to a snowbank. The cab driver got out of his car and discovered the injured poodle. The shepherd stood above her wagging his tail. After he picked up the small dog and put her in his car he looked around for the shepherd, but he had gone.

Dr. W. F. Sturgill was a physician for the Norfolk and Western Railroad. He also owned several fine dogs and was president of the National Foxhunters Association. He treated a friend's dog for an injury suffered on barbwire. Approximately a year later Dr. Sturgill heard a scratching on his door. He opened the door to discover his friend's dog, but with him was another dog with injured and bleeding paws. The doctor took care of the injuries and the dogs trotted off together.

Another story told by the Gaddises is of a bighorn sheep who during the summer of 1962 came down from the high country to the town of Mt. Baldy, California. The ewe was very sick. She was found and nursed back to health by a doctor. Once well, she returned to the mountains. But two months later she brought her ailing newborn lamb to the doctor's home. Unable to heal the lamb herself, she had come back to the man who could help.

Confronted with a growing body of knowledge that destroys old theories regarding the restrictive nature of instinct, that animals were unable to reason, and so on, we must rethink our concepts of animal nature. The old models will not suffice.

Will our new knowledge provide us with greater respect for other life forms than our own? Will we gain a new kind of reverence for all of life? If we do, in what ways will this affect our lives? Will our new awareness and sensitivity demand different sources of food protein than meat? Will the day of the hunter soon end? Organizations have been formed to protect the seals, the wolves, coyotes, dolphins, whales, certain birds—will this movement grow?

What does the possible extinction of a species mean to us? How might it affect our lives? Scientist Jacques Cousteau has stated that unless we quickly learn to take care of our oceans they will be dead in not too many years. Others have suggested that the demise of life in the seas is soon followed by death on land. Such possibilities are another reason for gaining a greater understanding of animals. Oceanographer John Todd speaks of this need for knowledge. He is quoted by Michael Schofield in an article, "The Smelly Factor," written for *Smithsonian* magazine, as saying: "The oceanographic community has begun to realize the urgency of acquiring knowledge of how marine animals communicate. This is no longer purely an academic or scientific matter. The languages of animals are the means whereby they organize their lives in relation to each other—just as we do. Their communication is crucial to their survival, but the language of fish and other marine creatures probably represent the weakest link in their life histories. Their signals can be jammed or disrupted by extremely low levels of pollutants, and this could have a catastrophic effect on their social behavior. What I am saying is that insidious levels of pollution can alter social behavior in such a way as to prevent there even being a next generation."

Karl-Erik Fichtelius and Sverre Sjolander call for a change in man's attitudes toward the animal kingdom in their closing remarks in their book *Smarter Than Man*?: "Even people who understand the doctrine of evolution intellectually have a hard time feeling strongly enough that man is a part of the living earth. Man needs something to shake him to his roots, to impress him deeply with the fact that he does not own the earth. This some-thing, which might give man the humility he needs, could be a greater knowledge of the other large-brained ani-mals.''

The suggestion that man does not own the earth pre-sents us with a somewhat startling perspective. We have for some time believed that if a nation could take and hold a body of land, its citizens could claim ownership. Once having ownership we believed—outside of certain restric-tions affecting other landowners—we could do anything we wished with the land. It was ours to plow, plant, burn, flood, or place buildings on. Only humans had anything to say about it. No other life form was consulted or given any thought. If animals were involved at all, it was either to work the land or to be a part of the product produced. Now we have to ask if man alone has the right to judge how the earth is to be used. Does my title to the land provide me with greater rights than the animals that live and depend on it? Is man's survival and pleasure the only question of consequence? Are these questions fanciful, or do they have some significance? Do animals have any rights?

Down through the ages not all human beings were rec-ognized as having rights. Sovereignty has often been lim-ited to royal heads, dictators, etc., who alone determined the extent of rights held by others. Control still remains in the hands of a few in most nations today. The right to vote remained the privilege of adult males until recent years, and not too long ago the males had to be property owners and of a certain race. For centuries, women, slaves, and to some extent children were chattel or property to be disposed of according to the whims of the owner. This is largely the position that animals are in today. Will animal rights ever become an issue? Likely this will depend on what we learn about other creatures than ourselves, what their position—along with ours—is in the universe. A little more than a century ago a slaveowner would have scoffed if asked if slaves had rights. Is the question regarding an-imals ridiculous? Will it always remain so?

In his book *Man and Dolphin*, Dr. Lilly wonders what will happen if the dolphin achieves a bilateral conversational level. He suggests that if this should happen, the dolphin will become an ethical, legal, and social problem. "Then," he states, "they will have reached the threshold of humanity, as it were . . . if they reach the conversational abilities of any normal human being, we are in for trouble. Some groups of humans will then step forward in defense of these animals' lives and stop their use in experimentation: they will insist that we treat them as humans and that we give them medical and legal protection. If the means of their further education in humanity is available, there probably will be an explosive development of such education."

Some may ask why this concern for animals when so many humans are oppressed and starving. Any argument that this book has put forth for the respect, appreciation, and protection of animals does not intend in any sense to minimize human problems—and they are many—nor in any manner to distract our attention from high-priority concerns.

But if our considerations of animals were directed only to the welfare of mankind alone, the priority would be reasonably high. This reason is not from the standpoint of balances in nature, nor from the roles animals play in our food production. The issue is greater than these: Our treatment of animals is important to our own internal states. If we are to expand our horizons, to grow, to understand what the new physics means by the relatedness of each and every living thing, then our love and appreciation of all life is essential. In a world where feelings and thoughts are things, our respect and reverence for all living things will be reflected in our own being.

Bibliography

Asimov, I. *Asimov's Guide to Science*. New York: Basic Books, 1972.

Boone, J. A. *Kinship with All Life*. New York: Harper & Brothers, 1952.

Bradley, D. and R. A. *Psychic Phenomena*. West Nyack, N.Y.: Parker Publishing Co., 1967.

Brown, B. *ESP with Plants and Animals*. New York: Essandess Special Editions, 1971.

Burton, M. *The Sixth Sense of Animals*. New York: Taplinger, 1973.

Castaeneda, C. *The Teachings of Don Juan: A Yaqui Way of Knowledge*. New York: Ballantine Books, Inc., 1969.

Cerminara, G. *Many Lives, Many Loves*. New York: William Sloane Associates, 1963.

————. "Missie, the Psychic Dog of Denver," *Psychic*, September–October 1973.

Dorst, J. *The Migrations of Birds*. Quoted in Copley News Service Feature, June 2, 1968.

Droscher, V. *The Friendly Beast*. New York: E. P. Dutton & Co., Inc., 1971.

Dunlap, J. *Exploring Inner Space*. New York: Harcourt, Brace and World, 1971.

Eckstein, G. *Everyday Miracle*. New York: Harper & Brothers, 1940.

Edwards, Frank. *Strange World*. New York: Lyle Stuart, Inc., 1964.

Emlen, J. T., and Penny, R. L. *Scientific American*, October 1966.

Fichtelius, K. E., and Sjolander, S. *Smarter Than Man?* New York: Ballantine Books, 1974.

Fodor, N. *Between Two Worlds*. West Nyack, New York: Parker Publishing Co., 1964.

————. *Encyclopedia of Psychic Science*. New Hyde Park, N.Y.: University Books, 1966.

Gaddis, V. and M. *The Strange World of Animals and Pets*. New York: Cowles Book Company, Inc., 1970.

Ghali, P. Chicago Daily News Service, October 18, 1958.

Haggard, R. *Proceedings*, British Society for Psychical Research, October 1904.

Heindel. *The Rosicrucian Cosmo-Conception*. Oceanside, Calif.: Rosicrucian Fellowship, 1911.

Hix, E. *Strange as It Seems*. New York: Doubleday & Co., 1953.

Hole, C. *Haunted England*. London: B. T. Batsford Ltd., n.d.

Isaacs, G. N. "Magic Zoology in the British Isles," *Tomorrow Magazine*, Summer 1953.

Kerrell, B., and Goggin, K. *The Guide To Pyramid Energy*. Santa Monica, Calif.: Pyramid Power V, Inc., 1975.

Lilly, J. *Man and Dolphin*. Garden City, N.Y.: Doubleday & Co., 1961.

Lorenz, Konrad. *King Solomon's Ring*. New York: Time Inc., 1962.

Mead, D. *Science Digest*, March 1976.

Michell, J. *The View over Atlantis*. New York: Ballantine Books, 1969.

Monroe, R. *Journeys Out of the Body*. New York: Doubleday, 1973.

Morris, R. L. "Animals and ESP," *Psychic*, October 1973.

Neihardt, J. G. *Black Elk Speaks*. New York: Pocket Books, 1972.

O'Donnell, E. *Animal Ghosts*. London: Rider & Co., n.d.

Ostrander, S., and Schroeder, L. *Psychic Discoveries Behind the Iron Curtain*. Englewood Cliffs, N.J.: Prentice-Hall, 1970.

Packard, V. *Animal I.Q.* New York: Dial Press, 1950.

Palmer, J. D. *Natural History*, March 1966.

Papashvily, G. and H. *Dogs and People*. Philadelphia: J. B. Lippincott Co., 1954.

Peterson, J. "Lessons from the Indian Soul," *Psychology Today*, May 1973.

Pierrakos, J. "The Energy Field in Man and Nature," Institute of Bioenergetic Analysis, n.d.

Roark, E. *Just a Mutt*. New York: Whittlesey House, 1947.

Rucks, L. *Oaklahoman and Times*, April 24, 1976.

Schofield, M. "The Smelly Factor," *Smithsonian*, August 1972.

Schul, B., and Pettit, E. *The Psychic Power of Pyramids*. Greenwich, Conn.: Fawcett Publications, 1976.

————. *The Secret Power of Pyramids*. Greenwich, Conn.: Fawcett Publications, 1975.

Storer, D. *Amazing but True Animals*. Greenwich, Conn.: Fawcett Publications, 1963.

Stromberg, G. *Man, Mind and the Universe*. Los Angeles: Science of Mind, 1973.

Szilard, L. *The Voice of the Dolphin and Other Stories*. New York: Simon and Schuster, 1961.

Waite, D. V. "Do Animals Really Possess a Sixth Sense?," *Probe the Unknown*, May 1975.

Walker, D. *Spooks Deluxe: Some Excursions into the Supernatural*. New York: Franklin Watts, Inc., 1956.

Watson, L. *Supernature*. New York: Doubleday, 1973.
Williams, J. H. *Elephant*.
Wilson, E. O. "Pheromones," *Scientific American*, 1963.

Index